FREEDOM
—— AND ——
INTERIM
MINISTRY

FREEDOM
—— AND ——
INTERIM
MINISTRY

12 Freedoms Of The Interim

By
John Helgeson

ARPress
ILLUMINATING IDEAS
EMPOWERING VOICES

ARPress
45 Dan Road Suite 36
Canton MA 02021

Hotline: 1(888) 821-0229
Fax: 1(508) 545-7580

Ordering Information:
Quantity Sales. Special discounts are available on quantity purchases by corporations, associations, and others. For details, contact the publisher at the address above.

Printed in the United States of America.

ISBN-13   Paperback   979-8-89356-594-2
                 eBook   979-8-89356-596-6
                 Hardback   979-8-89356-595-9

Library of Congress Control Number: 2024903105

To my wife Nancy for her support
and to all interim ministers

Table of Contents

Introduction

I have been both an interim minister and what is called a regular installed minister. Without a doubt in mind, I say that the interim minister has much more freedom than the regular installed minister. A regular installed minister or pastor is focal to a congregation. For both the congregation itself and the community of which that congregation belongs, the regular installed minister is the person everyone sees as central, as basic, as crucial to the life of the congregation. Often, for better or worse, the congregation is defined by who is the regular installed minister.

When a congregation has a regular installed minister, it is seen as having a stability it does not have when there is no regular installed minister in place. An interim minister is deliberately transitory, one who will go when the regular installed minister comes. Precisely because of that temporary status, the interim minister has more freedom than any regular installed minister. The stability, centrality, and focus that belong to a regular installed minister ultimately limit the pastor's freedom. A temporary pastor, as the interim is, knows time is limited and thereby can act promptly, decisively, and clearly in situations.

A regular installed minister or pastor has the luxury of time and can wait out situations. The ultimate waiting out is waiting for a tough member to die so that change can come about. But to deal with explosive situations, the waiting out may only make the situations worse, and dealing efficiently and promptly in such situations usually has significant side effects. The most common is that people leave the church as a result of having chosen sides, and the pastor's side was not chosen by these people. Thus, many regular installed ministers instead let issues slide and thereby let them fester. An interim can deal promptly and effectively with these situations because the binds on the regular installed pastor are not there. The interim will be gone, but the interim will be able to clean up the mess before the regular installed minister is in place.

I would suggest the most important role for an interim is to be able to take on the messes lingering in a congregation and clean them up. An interim is put in position to make it possible for the church to move from its previous pastor to its new pastor. And the new pastor will not be a clone or exact duplicate of the pastor previously there. Thus, the interim has to make it possible for change to come about in the interim time, or the new pastor is not going to last.

To be honest, every regular installed pastor leaves messes behind that need to be cleaned up before the new pastor is in place. The alternative is the regular installed pastor becoming an unintentional interim. The minister will have to do interim work and thereby not function as a regular installed pastor. Worse, by doing that unintentional interim work, the so-called regular installed minister will not last long. Therefore, the interim who takes the job seriously will indeed clean up those messes, no matter what it takes. And that is freedom, pure and simple.

I have served as an interim minister voluntarily and involuntarily. In other words, I am now an interim minister because I want to be an interim minister. However, in one church I served as that regular installed pastor, I wound up doing the work of the interim minister. In that church I was the unintentional interim. And after a while, because I was supposed to be the regular installed pastor, it got to me. I had enough and left. Ironically, in God's good time and at God's calling, I came back to that time and found myself being led into interim ministry. Now I am deliberately cleaning up messes in churches, thus making it possible for the next minister to function fully in a stable environment.

For the sake of this book, I have defined twelve freedoms an interim minister has and how they function. These are freedoms I personally know and can relate to. There may be other freedoms an interim has, but I am convinced these are basic to the role of an effective interim. Each chapter will deal in depth with each of these freedoms.

These freedoms an interim pastor or minister have, in no particular order (though for convenience I will present them sequentially in chapters), are speech, worship, to act, to disagree, to override or veto, to heal, to explain, to terminate, to change, to experiment, to leave, and to hope. How important each freedom will be is determined by the need of the church the interim minister is serving. At certain churches, not all of these will be emphasized, while at other churches, others will be emphasized. An interim has to be committed to freedom in order to function well in a church in transition. One should not be an interim unless one can work in an environment where freedom is central.

As I have put together this book, I have discovered that in considering the interim's freedoms, I have also explored ministry from an interim's perspective how an interim sees ministry. The freedoms of an interim have a lot to say about ministry in general and installed or regular ministries in particular.

1

The Freedom of Speech

Of course, every pastor or minister has freedom of speech when it comes to the pulpit. But the real question is, how many clergy actually say to the congregation what they really want to say? I am willing to say that only a few do. We even have a term for it—prophetic preaching, or in the old days, hellfire-and-damnation preaching. Nowadays, most preachers are very diplomatic in their preaching. Yes, we talk about sin and all of that, but in general, abstract, nonpersonal ways. Heaven forbid the preacher became too specific, or that preacher would not last long!

Take this one step further. How many installed pastors speak to the congregation or specific people in the congregation in ways that need to be spoken? No doubt there are some, but they are not in the numbers they should be. Irritate people in the congregation, and watch everything break loose. Of course, there are ministers who are very good at saying what needs to be spoken through the use of cryptic language. They tell stories, updated parables, or hypothetical situations, among other types of preaching, to say what needs to be said.

In the literary world, this happens regularly in science fiction, fantasy, and allegorical writing. With preachers, it is the art of hiding the obvious behind the imaginative or the mysterious. And the preacher hopes those who need to hear get the point. However, that is exactly the problem; those who need to hear will not get the point, unless someone is blunt and undiplomatic. In other words, some people have to be told in no uncertain terms what they are doing is wrong or at least a problem for the church.

Very few clergy are willing to do that. It somehow smells of being un-Christian or something like that. How can you tell the truth in love without hurting someone's feelings or provoking hostility in response? So instead, a situation just sits there and gets worse unless someone explodes. Then the fire cannot be put out, and like a house after a fire, it requires a great deal of reclamation, and it is not the same as before the fire.

This is where the interim can and should function. An interim being transitory can and should be the person who can speak what everyone knows needs to be said and said clearly. An interim can preach clearly. Even more, an interim can speak the unspeakable, name the unnamable, and thus make it possible for people to finally deal with an underlying problem in the church.

Speaking to Toxic People

Sometimes, there are toxic people in the congregation. They figuratively poison the congregation. They may be and usually are very active people in the congregation. As a result, the congregation does not want to confront them or even talk about them. These people are creating all types of problems in the church, but no one is willing to do anything about them.

Enter the interim. The interim has no ties to the congregation and is there in the name of Jesus Christ to help a congregation move on. And if a person (or persons) is holding the church back, the interim needs to talk the talk that can finally solve the problem.

It may actually be speaking to that person bluntly, frankly, and honestly. Paul from a distance did this with the church at Corinth. I wonder if he could have done it if he had been on the scene at Corinth for some time. He always valued his freedom to not be tied down to a congregation, though he started congregations, helped congregations from afar, wrote regularly to congregations about how to deal with their problems, and sent people to follow up.

An interim is on the scene for a period of time and has only a limited amount of time to deal with situations. Therefore, an interim can preach clearly. An interim can devise situations and devices that force the congregation to break the silence and start speaking out about problem people. And yes, there are times the interim will be the full-scale lightning rod needed to ground the church through the fury that is waiting to explode.

By virtue of that transitoriness, an interim can speak to people who need to be spoken to. Even more, there are times the interim may be the one person who can handle the situation once and for all. In the worst-case scenario, the interim may be the one who has to ask a person to leave the church. Hopefully, the interim will have enough skills to do it gracefully and positively for all concerned, but there are no guarantees. More about this will be said in the chapter on the freedom to terminate.

Yes, there may be side effects like other people being hurt because of the problem person being removed; just like in surgery, removing a body part creates issues, but rather the issues than the destruction of the body. And yes, someone has to say the truth and let the words be spoken for the healing of the church. Thus, an interim is the best positioned to do so.

Openness

If the past pastor has been a problem, the interim should allow the people to speak that openly and publicly. They need to have the freedom to hear those words from each other, and as a result, they are free to deal with whatever it takes to ensure such a situation does not happen again. The interim says the words everyone knows and encourages everyone else to say them as well.

Nothing is hidden. Everything is exposed. Problems are brought to the light. Remember that Jesus is the light of the world. He is also the truth. And the truth shall set you free, while dark secrets keep you bound. Problem people keep a church bound in the past, tied to the past, staked to the past, and enchained until the bonds are broken.

Speaking what needs to be spoken, saying what needs to be said, and allowing the words to be heard opens a church to a freedom it cannot have if everything is buried, ignored, or rationalized. Some people only need to hear the words told to them, and they repent.

They change. They realize what they have done, and they become the Christians they were always meant to be.

Instead of a person or persons, the problem that needs to be spoken about may be an ongoing situation in the life of the church. Let's face it. There are churches uncomfortable with evangelism, children, older adults, neighborhood ministries, casual dress, tattoos, college students, or any of a number of other matters churches must deal with regularly.

Who if not the interim is going to get a church to talk about these issues? Who if not an interim is going to ask why these are problems? Who if not the interim is going to say out loud that these problems need to be faced? This does not mean the interim is going to solve all the church's problems. It does mean the interim gets the church to talk about these issues and thereby makes it possible for a regular pastor to follow through on these issues and resolve or at least deal successfully with these issues.

Call the interim the designated talker of the congregation, if you like. The interim has the freedom to talk about what is causing problems in the congregation or for the congregation. Whether it is demographics or changing times, the interim keeps up with the times and with the faith and can speak comprehensively about how they impact the church.

The knowledge an interim has is thereby passed on to the congregation that needs it. The interim speaks, and the congregation hears. The interim may do this one-on-one in casual conversation, or it may happen in very formal forums called specifically to discuss the issue. The interim may speak to leaders in the congregation and thereby encourage them to act officially. Or the interim may speak to a congregation in preaching about such an issue, and thereby let someone who hears follow through.

In other words, there are many ways an interim can influence, help, and/or free a church by speaking out. The interim sees the issue and speaks out to those who need to hear and those who are able to make a difference. Preaching is more than just what is said from the pulpit, but anyone who discounts the pulpit for preaching does not understand the church or human nature.

Preaching

Consider preaching. The best interim ministers use preaching to speak to the congregation in the name of Jesus Christ, and that means to the congregation specifically. I have known all types of preaching techniques used from the pulpit or, for that matter, moving out of the pulpit while preaching. The techniques are just that, techniques to help the word be heard. What works for one preacher may not work for another. By the same token, some techniques will only work in certain churches, but not in others. But a preacher being honest and true is heard by a congregation, regardless of the technique used.

If we really believe the Bible is the word of God, and I do, then the interim can allow the word of God to be spoken to the congregation in ways that help them through times of transition. One way is for the interim to find and use passages in Scripture that deal with transitions and allow them to speak. For example, churches in transition are uneasy, even fearful. A great text I have used early in my interim positions is the first nine verses of chapter 1 of Joshua. After all, Joshua was afraid. He felt he was no Moses, whom he succeeded, and he knew he really needed God's assurance in a new situation. Thus, God says to Joshua, "As I was with Moses, so I will be with you; I will not fail you or forsake you" (1:5). God then uses a line that is stated three times in the remaining verses: "Be strong and courageous" (1:6, 7, 9). Indeed, to finish this text, the point is clear: "Be strong and courageous; do not be frightened or dismayed, for the Lord your God is with you wherever you go" (1:9).

Then and only then (1:10) does Joshua go into action. I point out to churches in transition that they too need to be strong and courageous. They need not be afraid. God is with them. I understand their fears, their insecurities, their unease, and their doubts at such a time, and that is why God has sent me there. God, through me as interim, is working to lead them onward into a new future, like Joshua led the people beyond Moses. I am leading them beyond their previous pastor into a new tomorrow under God's guidance.

This text I use as a sermon, but I also refer to it in conversations, and I can see it being used in Sunday school classes or as a devotion to beginning church board meetings. It is a text that demands to be spoken to the people by the interim, and I do so speak it. There are other texts as well that interims can and have used to speak to the situation. The interim has the freedom to find and use those texts.

If the pastor more specifically follows the lectionary, there are numerous texts useful to speak freely to the fears, doubts, insecurities, and unease that permeate a time of transition. Advent texts on waiting for the Lord, to cite one example, are great to define the need for patience at such moments and the fact that the Lord is in charge of the time we are waiting. A good, creative interim will easily find many texts helpful to the interim process, and then will speak them to the congregation in whatever setting makes sense.

In Conclusion

I have only begun to mine the idea of how the freedom of speech the interim has works. The interim can explain to the church what is needed. The interim can eloquently explain what the congregation is dealing with. The interim can become the voice of the congregation as it seeks to define its future. The interim has the freedom to speak the words that need to be spoken.

And the interim allows others the freedom to speak, making sure their voices are heard and not stifled. By providing voices to the otherwise voiceless, the church hears all its people, and in doing so makes the church truly live in Jesus Christ for all people. The church is given a voice through the interim, and that freedom to provide a voice makes a church live in all people.

Of course, that freedom to speak must be taken responsibly. If it is not, it will fail the church, even ultimately lose the church. In other words, no interim should live for sarcasm, viciousness, mean-spiritedness, nastiness, and other types of speech that continually, regularly, constantly put people down. This freedom to speak is a tool, and like all tools must be used responsibly. Yet used wisely under God's guidance and after prayerful consideration, it is a gift to the church in a time of transition. It opens the future for the church in Jesus Christ.

2

The Freedom of Worship

Anyone who regularly attends a worship service of a church where the installed pastor has been in place for a number of years knows the style of worship the pastor favors or uses. Even in the most liturgical churches, a pastor has a certain way of doing worship that is distinctly the pastor's. After all, each of us is unique, and worship leadership is bound to be unique to the person leading it. Another way to say it is to use the old cliché that we are creatures of habit.

Liturgy as Pattern of Worship

Naturally, the habits of worship depend on what the church means to convey in worship and how the pastor fits into that pattern. Liturgy is the pattern of worship, and even the most nonliturgical or free churches use a pattern of worship that can be followed by those who regularly attend. Every church gets in a habit of how it will do worship, and that habit becomes a pattern, which is its liturgy.

In highly liturgical services, the liturgy and what it says is important. A pastor or minister in such a situation leads the flow of the service in ways that are unique to the pastor. In free services, emotions and feelings are important to be expressed. A pastor or minister in such a situation leads the church members to fully express themselves in such a situation. The pastor does this in ways that come out of the particular personality of the clergy.

If worship could be seen along a line, highly liturgical would be on one side of the line and free services on the other. Obviously, many churches, if not most, would be somewhere in between. Regardless of the church's location on the line, the minister has to function within the parameters set for the church. The minister in that setting has been trained to fit within the church's dimensions. Yet each minister is still unique and brings personal perspectives or style into that setting. No two ministers would do a service the same way, no matter how organized the service was.

Messing Up the Pattern

Along comes an interim, and the best interims mess up the pattern. Notice I said the word mess, which an interim is cleaning up. However, sometimes an interim must create a mess in order to get the church's attention, especially when the church has become staid or stale. Indeed, the worship may have become so habitual as to be meaningless or just something people do without thinking. Worship has to speak to people and involve the people at some level, in some way. If it does not, it has gone stale.

The interim may well see that the worship, as central to a church as it is, has become a problem. It is no longer meeting the needs of the congregation. When that happens, the interim must mess up the pattern and offer alternatives. Some will stick; some will not. The church must decide after the interim tries them on the congregation. Some of this will be a matter of experimenting on the congregation, a topic I will discuss in a later chapter.

For now though, the interim in such matters has the freedom of worship. This means the freedom to make worship more relevant, more meaningful, more appropriate, more spiritual, more denominational, more free, and the list could go on and on, depending on the needs of the congregation. There are any number of ways this can happen, from the simplest to the most innovative, again depending on the congregation and how the interim sees the congregation's needs.

For example, the interim may simply read Scriptures more dramatically, or in a different setting may use acoustical enhancements. Perhaps the Scriptures will be sung or chanted. The congregation may be involved responsively in the reading of Scripture, or perhaps a number of people will read. The congregation can be allowed to offer its prayers, or prayers can be read from different vantage points.

In liturgical prayers, they can be presented in such a way that the congregation is not just a silent witness.

Whatever happens in worship can be examined to see if it is helpful or not and whether it is speaking to the people. In liturgical settings where the service is established, how the elements are presented will determine if they are doing what they need to do. There are always ways to enhance what is done in worship, so that even the most common elements of worship do not become rote. The Lord's Prayer can be sung by the congregation. The type of music sung needs to be examined and seen if it is reaching the people. If not, try other types of music.

Evaluating Worship

Sometimes, an interim will need to survey the congregation and find out where the worship is working and where it is not. Everything from timing to presentation to variety to doing things in worship never done before may be necessary to ensure the worship worships for the people. Is the praise praise? Is the offering offering? Is the prayer prayer? Or is the congregation just going through the motions? The worship must speak to the people where they are.

The interim is short-term and thus can have the congregation look at its worship and decide what is meaningful and what is not. To prepare for a new pastor, the interim can lead a congregation through an evaluation of its worship and institute changes that make sense to the congregation.

In churches with a formal pattern of worship, sometimes, if allowed, worship order changes. Moving around the elements of the worship while keeping the same format may get people to realize what is involved in worship. It used to be quite common for worship services to end with preaching. Now it is less common, but still out there. Maybe the placement of the preaching will open people up to a new understanding that preaching is not all that is involved in worship, or even that it is the most important element in worship.

If churches have been singing their canon of hymns (in other words, the same hymns over and over), it is time for the interim to have a hymn of the month to allow the congregation to learn new hymns. For those churches with hymnals, the interim may push for new hymnals or new styles of singing hymns (it may mean screens or other audio-visual and computer-generated equipment). For those already into the "contemporary" scene, it may mean reclaiming traditional hymns, even if they are jazzed up a little. Interestingly, what is called "emergent" or "emerging" worship insists on all types of music and all types of styles. I believe that is a possibility all types of churches can and should explore under the guidance of interims, who can and will work in this field.

Neutrality

I would expect a good interim to be aware of all that is going on in worship today. And an interim cannot be judgmental about the types of worship out there, but rather must be neutral and willing to explore with a congregation the various possibilities. Now, anyone who knows anything about the word *neutrality* will understand that neutrality is not apathy or ignorance, nor is it anything that disregards what is happening. For that matter, neutrality is quite active in ensuring its neutrality. In the political sphere, neutral countries are proactive, thoughtful, and often very involved in the world.

Using that analogy for worship, a neutral interim works within the system of worship in place and offers ways to enhance it. Where that leads is open to God's calling for the church. By being proactive, a neutral interim can open a church to what is happening elsewise in the world of worship. For some churches, this will mean using contemporary elements; for others it will mean using traditional elements. The interim is not biased *for* any type of worship, nor does the interim criticize any type of worship. The interim believes in worship and accepts the patterns a congregation chooses while seeking to make it speak to the congregation.

The worst thing an interim can do is to try to *impose* a style of worship on a congregation that is not natural to that congregation. An interim can open a congregation to seeing what is out there in worship, but cannot impose it on the congregation or try to make the congregation think as the interim thinks. The freedom of the interim in worship is to get beyond the so-called worship wars or to transcend the patterns of worship. The interim is only interested in worship as worship. Nothing but worship in a particular setting, namely the congregation where the interim is working, counts.

The interim will work with the system of worship in place in a congregation, or the interim will be a problem to the church instead of a help to a church. Unfortunately, as I have heard from churches and denominational leaders, not all interims take this advice seriously. An interim has freedom to enhance worship, but all freedoms come with responsibilities. And an interim who destroys the worship a congregation uses destroys the church and guarantees a failed interim.

In Conclusion

Explore worship with the congregation. Use the freedom you are given to lead worship and work in worship. Make worship speak to the congregation. Work with the congregation in worship. Thus, worship changes come naturally out of the congregation's understanding of worship as the interim leads the congregation. The congregation will give the clergy a freedom to work with the worship, and the interim will use that responsibly to lead the congregation where it needs to go and where it can handle going.

3

The Freedom to Act

How many churches procrastinate on issues they know need to be dealt with? How many churches don't act as they really know they should? How many churches are so tied into their own version of bureaucracy that they can't get things done as they need to be done? How many churches give in to those infamous seven last words of the church: "we've never done it that way before"? These are just several questions that point out how churches find ways not to act.

The results of not acting are at best (if you can call it that) stagnation or apathy, and at the worst death. Some denominational leaders will do all in their power to have interims who are good at revitalizing churches that are stagnant or near death put in those situations. To use a cliché, it is the hope these interims will give the church a swift kick in the pants. The churches will start doing what they are supposed to be doing. They will wake up. They will become churches.

Such churches can be just going through the motions, but they are not really functioning as churches. Some churches can be so ingrown or so self-focused that they cannot see the bigger picture about the church. Some churches are so into survival mode they cannot see beyond themselves.

The interim has the freedom to act in all of these situations because there are no long-term ties that can entwine regular or installed pastors. Indeed, I would go so far as to declare that an interim who does not get the church to act is not being an interim. Churches expect interims to act. Churches expect that the interim will get the church to act, no matter how painful it may entail.

Doing What Needs to Be Done

Usually, an interim will find that there have been issues just sitting around seemingly forever. Everyone knows they need to be acted upon, but the will is not there, or someone is not able to push them through. Therefore, the good interim will not let those issues continue but will find ways to get them done. The interim may have to bring groups together, committees together, or certain people together, all with the expressed goal of making sure this is done. Indeed, the interim will not allow them to procrastinate on these issues any longer, but will keep prodding and pushing until the issues are dealt with. After the issues are dealt with, it is actually common to see a sigh of relief from the congregation that finally the issues have been dealt with.

On the positive spin, churches that are growing will finally deal with increasing staff, whether administrative, janitorial, worship-related, youth, or even ordained. The church knows it needs to happen but cannot quite get the will to do so. The interim can push that issue and have it happen. I have seen committees and groups hem and haw, sometimes deliberately, sometimes unconsciously, over staff additions that everyone knows are needed. I push and prod and lead them to making the decisions they know need to be made. I do not let them postpone, but I keep them on point, showing what they already know and helping them to move when the natural inclination is to stall. Just having that one voice, that one person who makes sure they follow through, is usually enough to break the logjam and get the staff needed.

Everyone needs leadership. The leadership of an interim is geared to making things happen, to doing what needs to be done, to ensuring that actions are not left hanging. Sometimes it will be by supportive words. Other times, it may be innovative leadership that works with people where they are and enables them to make the decisions they need to make. Occasionally, the interim will simply have to take charge and be the person who does whatever it takes to get an action done. The interim has to lead in such a way that it will make a difference.

Play to Strength

There are churches that commonly wind up doing the wrong thing for the church. As people are unique, churches are unique. Each church has special talents, special gifts, even strengths that the people and often the community associate with a particular church. Hence, a church may be well noted for its mission work. Another church may be a beacon for the community, where many community activities arise from the church. Some churches are known for their innovative worship. Other churches are known for their intensive pastoral care. There are churches that specialize in small-group settings.

Is the church playing to its strength? Or is the church playing to its weaknesses or, perhaps I should say, what is not natural for the church? Some people in churches insist that since, as an example, their church is not a phenomenal mission church, it should pay less attention to what it is doing well to focus more on missions. Or if the church is gifted in worship but not doing as much in small-group settings, it should refocus on small-group settings.

The list of perceived weaknesses in the church, what the people of the church see as the church's weaknesses, are really not always weaknesses. Sometimes, indeed more often than most churches are willing to admit, there are things the church does not do well because they are really not what the church is about. They are not natural to the church. Therefore, when the church jumps on something alien or not natural to the church, it backfires on the church.

The interim can help a church to see what fits the church, what the church is all about, what is truly natural to the church. The interim becomes then a cheerleader for what makes the church special, unique, gifted. Indeed, the interim may push the church to act on those areas where it is at its best, and leading it away from those areas where it really does not make sense to the congregation.

Getting the church to act on its gifts becomes essential to the identity, the reality, and for that matter, the future of the church. Where the church is special, the interim must emphasize, focus, uplift, and cheer on those attributes. Put extra time and energy into them because they define the church and show the church at its best. They make the church what that church is. Now this does not mean ignoring everything else, since some churches put off dealing with anything where there are problems. A church must act where it needs to act, but a church cannot ignore what it is about in order to do something it is uncomfortable with.

The interim will recognize what a church is about and work to ensure that whatever flows from that knowledge will enhance the church. The materials about the church will say this. The media about the church will proclaim this. The programs in the church will demonstrate this. And the people in the church will live this. The interim will lead the church to act in ways that are natural to the church.

Church Bureaucracy

Another issue an interim will have to deal with is the church's bureaucracy. Too often bureaucracies get a bad name, but bureaucracies were set up to make things happen in recognizable ways. It is when the bureaucracy focuses on itself instead of its task that it becomes a problem and thus gives bureaucracies a bad name indeed. Good interims are politicians who know how to get things done within a defined system of government. Thus, the interim can know how to get the bureaucracy to act as it is intended to act, instead of how it sinfully acts.

Therefore, instead of letting the bureaucracy focus on itself, the interim has the bureaucracy focus on what it should be doing. As an example, if the mission committee has lost its mission work and is rather a mission committee in name and only blocking mission, it is time to lead that committee to fulfilling its function. If a women's organization founded on having women work in the church for God's good purposes has devolved into a social organization, it is time to lead those women to reclaim their identity. If the church's governing body has a seemingly endless number of rules or hoops anyone or any other group has to go through to get anything done, it is time for the interim to shake that body up and free it to act as a governing and not a blocking body.

The interim can use the bureaucracy to get things done. The interim will be trained politically to ensure the bureaucracy is not bureaucratic, but is serving the church. The bureaucracy is called to be a servant, as Jesus was a servant. And the interim will use political and biblical tools to ensure that the bureaucracy realizes it is part of the body of Christ to work with other parts of the body of Christ. Just as the body cannot be just an eye, it cannot be just a self-identifying bureaucracy that looks good on paper but does nothing for the good of the church of Jesus Christ. It is a tool. It is a body part. It is not everything in the church, but it is helpful to the church and necessary to the church. The interim works to use that bureaucracy for the service of the church of Jesus Christ.

Of course, there will be times the interim will have to reshape the bureaucracy. This involves all that is needed when reorganization is essential. I have known interims who have had to reshape committee structures of churches that were either ineffective or a negative influence on the church. Sometimes even the ruling boards have to be restructured. They may be too large for the size of the church. They may be trying to do too much work. Their length of meetings are too long. Too few people are overseeing too much. There may be no clear delineations of authority, and jurisdictional fights are common. Maybe one group does not trust another group. In other words, the structure has to be reshaped for the future of the church. And an interim who is good at restructuring is essential.

In Conclusion

Some churches deliberately build bureaucracies to ensure nothing gets done. I am here to say that cannot be allowed to continue. And when that resistance is broken down, the church functions, unless the seven last words of the church intervene. I cannot count how many times I have heard people in the church, who should know better, say, "We've never done it that way before." Sometimes churches have never done it that way before, but they need to do it that way regardless. If a church has a large number of youth and does not take the youth's desires into account, it is time. If a church has families with special needs that are not being met, it is time. On the other side, if a church has just been doing something because

the church has always done it that way, it is time to reconsider. Some things need to die if they are no longer serving their purpose. Certain groups may be just going through the motions and need to be allowed to die.

Tradition is a two-edged sword. It is a gift as it enables a church to understand itself and to make sense of where the church has been. It is a problem when it blocks change in the church and tries to put the church into a corner from which it cannot escape. The wise interim will be able to discern the difference and act appropriately. Continuing the analogy to a sword, it may take a "sword" to cut the bad of tradition away, the weeds of tradition that are blocking the church from dealing with church. The bad traditions have to be removed; the good traditions have to be reaffirmed. Tradition must be a tool for the good of the church. The interim can act to ensure tradition serves the church instead of stifling the church.

The interim time is a time for church to act. The interim can act in ways that have the church doing what it needs to be doing at this point in time and ensure that the church is moving and not being held back by its own inactions.

4

The Freedom to Disagree

How often can a regular pastor disagree with the congregation or ruling board? I expect the answer would be rarely, and that is only if the minister has built up a lot of good will that would allow the congregation or ruling board to tolerate disagreement. While pastors may encourage changes in directions in the congregation and get congregations to do things they have never done before, disagreement with the board or the congregation itself is hard.

Setting Up Pastors for Failure

At the most extreme, if a congregation wants to withdraw from the denomination but the minister does not, the minister's tenure is limited. On a different perspective, I knew of a minister deliberately hired to lead the congregation in mission who disagreed when the congregation forgot to mention that certain significant property matters had to be handled as well. That minister was let go. Indeed, numerous times ministers are hired with one expectation and discover, to their surprise, that certain other expectations in conflict with the main expectation arise. The result is usually short pastorates.

Sadly, certain churches are in effect pastor killers. They make it impossible for any pastor to function because they have built in so many conflicting expectations that no clergy could work within their church. Some churches really do not like or trust clergy, and therefore the people of the churches have devised their churches to be a minefield from which no pastor can escape. Just as Jesus was constantly challenged by the leaders of his day, so too the pastor is constantly challenged to the point that the minister becomes ineffective and leaves either voluntarily or involuntarily.

Then there are a number of churches facing the neighborhood crisis, meaning the church is located in a neighborhood from which it does not draw members. The members come from elsewhere to attend the church. A minister is called to bring in the neighbors only to discover that the present church members really do not want the neighbors in because they will change the very nature of the congregation.

There are all sorts of ways a congregation can set up a minister for failure. Unfortunately, the churches do not even understand that is what they are doing. They do not recognize that this is an innate problem. The church is the problem and not the minister. They are doomed to go through a series of ministers because they have made it impossible for any minister to function in their church. I will let you think through the implications of the words "their church."

Be that as it may, an interim minister may be their best hope, or at least the best hope of the denomination that wants to see such churches finally change for the better. In such circumstances, an interim is put in place to disagree and to change the mentality controlling such churches. The interim is not there for the long haul, but only long enough to make it possible for a minister to function. The threat of killing the pastor figuratively is not as effective when the interim is there precisely to end that system and has no long-term investment or desire to be in that church.

The freedom to disagree that the interim has is perhaps the strongest, even most provocative, freedom an interim has. The interim is going to move on anyway, and therefore is enabled to take on whatever is keeping the church from dealing with its pastors.

Confronting the Dysfunctional

Some churches fight having an interim because they sense or know that an interim will call their dysfunction (and I deliberately use that word) into question. I would suggest dysfunctional churches are most in need of an interim. Someone outside of the structure who does not have a tie to the church or certain people in the church is needed to see objectively what is going on and then suggest how to deal with the dysfunctionality. I have an interim friend who specializes in this type of ministry. Conflict training before going into such a dysfunctional setting is necessary. Being able to control people who have been controlling a congregation is important. Most likely, as in my previous chapter on the freedom to act, reorganization will be necessary because the dysfunction is built into the very structure of the church. Until that structure is changed to allow a church to move on, any pastor will not be allowed to function within the church.

An interim who knows how to disagree can lead a church into functioning as a church should function. Call this interim the stoplight, stopping traffic when it needs to be stopped. Only when it is safe to go on does the light change to green. The interim stops the dysfunction and only allows the church to go on when the church has moved beyond the dysfunction. The interim recognizes the problem and, by virtue of being an interim, does what is necessary to change or ultimately eliminate the problem. To change images, an interim in this situation is like a doctor breaking open a blister. It has to be done for the sake of the person, but it can be painful, and for a time, it can create a mess. If you have ever had a blister popped by a doctor, you know whereof I speak.

Call the interim disagreeing a blister popper, if you like. Whatever is holding the church back so that it cannot function brings about the interim to lance that blister. It may be the church as a whole. It may be certain members having inordinate powers. It may be certain groups in the church that have been allowed to become independent domains. Whatever makes the church dysfunctional has to be dealt with.

The level of these issues vary. Some can be quite small and easily handled. Others are so intertwined through the church that they are like a parasite and will require serious and precise work. Most are able to be handled by any good interim. The few where conflict is rife require those specialists I mentioned before.

Sensitivity

The problem these issues raise is the side effects. Or to remind ourselves of Jesus's parable, when the tares grow with the wheat, it requires special care that good wheat is not destroyed when removing the tares. In other words, the side effects of cleaning up this type of mess can be that good people will be lost, if the tares, the parasites, the blisters are not handled in ways that help and heal instead of ways that separate and destroy.

The interim's freedom to disagree has to include the responsibility to ensure good people are not hurt when cleaning up the mess. This requires sensitivity to people, realizing that people have ties even with difficult people that are difficult to let loose for the good of the congregation. An interim pastor may have to spend a great deal of time with people who feel their friends are being treated unfairly, despite the fact those friends are undermining the church. Pastoral care is essential, or good people are lost to the church.

When problem people need to be removed from leadership positions or from unofficial positions of power, they must be handled gingerly, cautiously, carefully. The best way is to make it possible for such people to see in themselves the need to step down. Some people, when shown tactfully the issues they create, will recognize the problem and step back. Other people will not see the issue once they are told point-blank. In those situations, the interim minister has to develop a cadre of people recognizing the problem and willing to agitate for the dismissal of that person.

In the most extreme situations, it may be necessary for the leadership of the church to discipline a member. Or if the church recognizes the problem but is uncomfortable with handling the person, the interim as the temporary authority can be the person to force the issue. I will deal with this later in the chapter on the freedom to terminate.

In Conclusion

In the cases where the institution must be disagreed with, the interim must be willing to work outside the formal structures of the church to reclaim it. If the board is the problem, work with those outside the board. If certain groups in the church are the problem, work with those outside the groups and ideally getting the officiating board to act as the officiating board it is supposed to be. There is always the case of the tail wagging the dog, where the board is totally ineffective because it allows someone or some someones to rule despite the governing board. In those cases, the board must be educated as to its duties and then empowered to act in the best interests of the church. And where the ruling body is the problem, ultimately, new leadership needs to be developed to take over the board and run the church responsibly.

The ability to disagree is crucial to the work of the interim. It makes a church be the church.

5

The Freedom to Override or Veto

Some pastors just want to get along. They allow themselves to be overridden on regular bases just because they want to get along and not cause fights. Eventually, they become mere figureheads at most for the church. Some churches like that type of pastor, but many come to realize that is no way to be a pastor. When that happens, the pastor is forced out and does not even realize what has happened or why.

Other clergy, in their desire to be loved or appreciated (a very human need), will allow difficult people to impose their will on the congregation. They become the best friends of these people, and these people then can say the minister agrees with me, and so must the church.

Those are just two examples among many more that could be cited where the minister is no longer an authority for the church, but rather at best a chaplain, and at worst, a nothing. Chaplains are absolutely essential clergy, as anyone in a nursing home, the military, hospitals, or various other intense situations can well attest. And every pastor must do chaplaincy duties. But if a pastor of a congregation is only a chaplain, that pastor is only dealing with a portion of the church's needs. Churches need administrators as well as chaplains. Indeed, churches need much more from a minister—whether preaching, teaching, leading worship, counseling, studying, etc. The list is long, and chaplain is part and parcel, but not the only responsibility.

Being a nothing is no help to a congregation. Someone who is just there and that is all, occupying space in the pastor's office but not being available, not working with groups and individuals, not having any input into the life of the church, and not making any waves lets the congregation go adrift. The ultimate reason for pastors, clergy, ministers, and priests is to lead a church in the way of the faith.

Administration

One of the givens of being a minister is to be an administrator, someone who is in charge of how the church functions and is willing to make decisions on how the church functions. It may be carrying out functions authorized by the church or its governing boards and making sure they are carried out appropriately. Anyone who keeps up with governments at all levels knows the need for competent administrators to carry out what the legislators authorized.

On the other hand, administrators often have to make decisions for the church, similar to CEOs of businesses. Usually, the church's clergy does not have as much authority or freedom as a CEO, but the buck has to stop somewhere, and the minister is that person. Incompetent administrators are the bane of a church's existence. The problems they create can entail the extremes of embezzlement to being audited by the IRS or being sued by a copyright holder. On a more mundane level are bad morale among staff, infighting among church leaders for power due to a vacuum at the top, lack of communication between the church office and the congregation, actions needing to be done are not, among a wide variety of other problems.

Bad administration is a genuine virus that sickens a congregation. Fortunately, most pastors are good administrators. However, even the good ones who have kept things under control are not necessarily able to oversee and properly override or veto all that must be overridden or vetoed. And therefore, when even the good ones move on, an interim will be needed to handle those situations where overriding or vetoing is absolutely essential.

Bad Ideas

Again, because of the duration of the interim, the interim has the freedom to override or veto what is clearly not in the best interests of the church. We may not have to go as far as Jesus when, after Peter recognized Jesus as the Son of God, and Jesus told him and the disciples that meant death, Peter tried to oppose Jesus, and Jesus had to call him Satan and to, in effect, get away. Yet churches, like every organization humans are involved with, can come up with bizarre ideas that are best buried on the spot. Humans being humans do not always recognize misguided ideas, even in churches. Someone must have the authority to say no, and the interim is that authority.

Interims have the freedom to fully override or veto really bad ideas, problem ideas, and yes, just downright dumb ideas. These ideas may have a life of their own and strong support for their implementation, but a good interim recognizes the problems with such ideas and vetoes them. As effectively as a governor or a president, the interim says no, and the no holds.

I realize purists will jump on this and say that unless the church has a hierarchical system in place, clergy do not have this authority at all. Indeed, there are boards that must make this decision or the church as a whole. Well, I have yet to see even the most democratic church not be swayed or even committed to following the clergy of the church. Specifically, if that clergy is absolutely opposed to some idea, it will fail, unless the church gets rid of the pastor on that issue. And yes, on significant issues, that does happen, as I have pointed out previously.

However, in most cases, all the minister has to say is no, and that no holds. For interim ministers, just by being in the position of being the clergy, the minister, the pastor in residence, even if temporarily, that authority is there as well. Indeed, the interim can take on the significant issues and veto them as well, if such issues would create too many problems for the church. Of course, if the interim takes on an issue that is central to the church and vetoes it, even the interim could be dismissed.

Nonetheless, there are all sorts of ideas that come up at churches, and some are beyond the pale. Hopefully, they will be recognized immediately and nipped in the bud. As an extreme example, a small church living in a small community and having but a limited income decides it wants to be a mega-church and build a humongous facility. I guarantee that to do so would at worst bankrupt the church, or at least leave the church with such a wide-open space that is not being used that the church would never recover. Reality must be the guide to determine what a church can and what a church cannot do. An interim well aware of the community's demographics would veto this and make sure it was buried forever.

The veto or overriding can be in done in many ways. Burying something behind a bureaucracy is one way. Holding hearings on controversial issues is another. Referring items to groups that meet irregularly can kill them. Allowing people to hear opposing views at public events or by providing "experts" showing the consequences will dampen any zeal for the project.

Sometimes just saying no will just do it. Or if those words come across too strong, there are diplomatic ways to override or veto problematic ideas. Be gentle. Be comforting. Offer alternatives. Redirect the energy for an idea into something more practical.

A good interim will find ways to override bad ideas. Sometimes just because an interim is in place, bad ideas pop out of a church. The church wants to do something about its perceived problems and thereby decides while the interim is there that anything that looks like it is solving the problem will work. Again, a reality check is important here. The interim can be positive, supportive, uplifting of the person proposing the idea, and at the same time ensuring that those ideas that are not helpful never are given the opportunities they do not deserve.

Staff and Filtering

Sometimes good administration itself will suffice and, in effect, veto or override problems. The staff recognizes there are certain issues the pastor is not going to accept, and such issues are overridden before they even reach the pastor. One of the great gifts an interim can do for the staff is to train them in the way of killing bad ideas they are presented with and ensuring they do not even reach the pastor.

As administrator, the pastor oversees the staff. An interim minister may have to help the staff to be the staff after bad interactions caused by the previous pastor. Just to increase staff morale, support staff, uplift staff, cheerlead staff is enough to ensure the administrative work the staff does is done well. And the staff will fully act as an intermediary between the church and the pastor, thus protecting the church from its own worst instincts.

Yet as administrator, a pastor is a filter. The best pastors know that things will come on their desks that need to be filtered out. Just like a filter helps heating units, air conditioners, and cars to function better while catching and eliminating what would inhibit their work, so does a pastor act in this way for a church. Many are the times an interim has to come into place just for this function. The church has not been filtering out the bad, the problematic, the distressing because the pastor has not taken on that responsibility. The interim's chief role may well be to filter out what has been holding back the church and providing the environment needed for the church to function appropriately.

This is just another metaphor for the interim vetoing what needs to be vetoed. There are any number of ways to say this. And an interim who recognizes this type of role will enable the church to become the church it wants to be and needs to be. That interim will open the church for a positive future built on what the church is about. That interim will allow the church to function as it was meant to function and as it wants to function.

In Conclusion

Yet I must say that an interim has to recognize where vetoes are needed and where they are not. An interim who comes in with veto pen heavily in hand does the church no good. An interim who comes to the church with an agenda and therefore will not allow the church to go in any direction except for the interim's bias is failing the church. The interim must be nonbiased, nonjudgmental, non-agenda oriented; in other words, as I have said previously, neutral, in the best sense of that term. Where vetoes come, they come naturally and necessarily without any bias on the part of the interim.

The freedom to veto that an interim has is a gift and a great responsibility. It can make a church finally be the church it is called to be. If used wisely, it really makes hope live in the church of Jesus Christ. If used badly, it causes problems for a church. It is important for the interim to use it responsibly and ably for the sake of the church. The church does live into the future when vetoes prevent disasters.

6

The Freedom to Heal

A beloved pastor dies while serving the church. A popular minister leaves the parish suddenly, unexpectedly. An effective clergy, who has made a real difference in the congregation, decides to quit ministry altogether. Due to major health issues, the good minister must resign. The most sensitive role of an interim is to heal those churches.

On the other hand, a minister is forced out. The pastor is discovered to have fingers in the financial cookie jar. The clergy are found to be engaged in sexual misconduct. The pastor comes to despise the church and lets the congregation know it. Ministers go out of their way to make life miserable in the congregation. The most sensitive role of an interim is to heal those churches.

Whether a pastor leaves on good terms or bad terms, whether unexpected factors or ongoing factors force a minister out of position, the fact is that an interim is essential in such situations. The interim may be the "counselor-in-chief" or "comforter-in-chief." The interim may need to lead people through the standard grieving processes because what has happened is "death" without the actual body. And where death physically has occurred, grief is only the beginning.

In all these situations mentioned so far and many others of a similar nature, healing is essential. Healing is necessary. A church that has made no movement toward healing after such situations is asking for disaster thereafter. You have to deal with the pain, whether one's personal or the church's collective. Indeed, an interim will deal with both, and sometimes they will be so intermingled that they complicate each other. A church cannot live in pain, grief, anguish, and all the other emotions that come in such situations.

A regular pastor doing this becomes an unintentional interim because healing the grief focuses on the past. A regular or installed clergy doing the healing in effect would just be reliving the past and would not be able to get beyond. That minister would not be able to function in the now, much less the future. Such a one would always be seen as the one who healed the past, and therefore could not have an effective ministry personally.

It is imperative an interim or its equivalent be put in place in such situations. Someone with the gift of healing is ideal for the work that must be done after disaster strikes the congregation. And those disasters are not just clergy-induced. A full-scale split in the church can be just as nasty and hard on a congregation as a pastor leaving under suspicious circumstances. Or if a church has endured a physical disaster (say a flood or a tornado, for example) and there is no pastor in place or the pastor is just leaving, healing will be essential.

Dealing with the Hurt

Regardless of the reason for the need to heal, an interim pastor put into such a situation must be willing to spend time with the congregation, especially those hurting. That hurt may be very open and, as a result, very angry. Or that hurt may be hidden and, as a result, very depressed. Add in the elements of grief, despair, hopelessness, fear, and so many other emotions, and the need for healing is essential for the health of the congregation. Indeed, if individually they are not healed, they surely will not be healed collectively as a congregation.

The interim will need to visit the people of the church who are hurting and in need of healing. Indeed, this is a good time to visit people in their homes, at their jobs, or making it a point to go where the people are and spend time with them. In all these occasions, make time for listening, time for praying, time for comforting, time for consoling, and time for just being present with the hurting person. The best pastoral skills will be necessary in such situations. In this matter, the clergy is a pastor. A pastor is one who truly is there with the people representing the Lord. A pastor becomes the Lord's presence to those needing healing.

Interims need to listen. The pain can come with anger. And it is appropriate and necessary for the interim to provide a pastoral presence whereby people can vent their anger at the situation. Sometimes, people will be angry with the one leaving or simply the fact a person left, even if the pastor is retiring. It is hard to give up on a person, and anger, even unjustified anger, is natural. Someone must listen to that anger and allow that anger to be expressed if there is to be healing. The anger cannot be allowed to sit, fester, and boil over in the congregant. It must be excised and removed. Thus, sometimes it just has to be allowed to explode like a volcano before the ground can settle around the person feeling the anger.

A pastor has to listen for the anger because the anger may also have a theological basis. It is very easy to get angry with God. One need only read Job or Jeremiah in the Bible to hear anger being expressed at God by Job and Jeremiah for what they endured, faced, put up with, or choose your word or emotion. Christians need to read Lamentations and a number of the Psalms asking God in anger why the country of which they were a part had to endure suffering. Why did they feel abandoned, set adrift, and left seemingly hopeless by the God they trusted and depended upon?

It works very similarly in people in churches who lose a pastor for whatever reason. I have heard church people wonder if God was mad at them because of what they went through as a result of the pastor's exit. They became angry with God and needed healing. They needed to know God was with them and cared for them. They needed a pastoral presence that could show the grace of God and listen to their anger.

The Loss of Church Buildings

There is a different dynamic when the church building itself is damaged or destroyed because of some disaster. Similarly, if the church itself has not been damaged or destroyed but their homes have, people grieve. We are constantly being told that buildings are just that, buildings and nothing more. If they go, they are just buildings after all.

Despite what we have heard, buildings locate us, buildings define us, buildings even make us. If we lose our homes, we lose something of our very own selves. We have made ourselves people who live in a home, and thereby understand ourselves by the homes in which we live. Take those away, and you take away an essential part of who we are.

In the same way, take away our churches (whether physically or otherwise), and you take away an essential part of our faith. We do define our faith in our physical churches. This is why it is extremely hard to have church move around and not have some fixed location or physicality. It may be a church building or it may be a space in a mall, but it is our holy space. Take that away, and we lose a spiritual dock. It has that type of mooring effect and that type of stability in the chaos waters of life.

People who lose homes or churches need to grieve. They need pastoral presences to help them deal with their real loss. A part of their identity has been physically removed from them, and it is hard to identify afterward. Sometimes in the building process that comes thereafter, as long as the people who have lost the building are involved, healing can come. Other times, the pastor must spend time, quality time, with such people to ensure them of the love of God amid the loss of what we loved in our homes and our churches. The interim in such situations must walk with the people, be with the people, lament with the people, and truly work with the people. Healing will not be easy, and people will never fully get over their loss. However, the good interim in such a situation can help the people to move forward and to integrate the loss into their own lives. They will see God's presence and love and be strengthened for the life still ahead.

The Need for Prayer

Christians in need of healing need pastors to pray for and with them. Interims coming into situations without pastors will find congregants needing someone to pray for their healing. It may be individually, or it may be collectively. It may be one-on-one praying with and for the person, including holding the person's hand or laying a hand on a shoulder or head. It may be collectively at worship, with prayers specifically mentioning the healing needed. It may be in group settings, as per boards or councils of the church, or committees or various other types of groups in the church. There may be the ruling board that needs prayer after what they went through. There may be certain groups in the church who experienced much pain and need healing prayer. The interim in such circumstances is to be the "pray-er" of the church.

By prayer, praying specifically, deliberately, evocatively for healing after what the church has endured, after what certain people have endured, and after what certain groups have endured is essential to healing. The power of the Holy Spirit becomes real in such prayers. I have many times seen people, groups, and churches lifted out of their pain, their anger, and other emotions by prayer. An interim must be a "pray-er," one who prays for the people, one whose prayers are for the people, and one whose prayers lead to healing the people.

Take this one step further. The best praying interims can lead a congregation in prayer for healing. This may include having special healing services for the congregation itself. The whole service is geared around prayer and healing in the name of the Lord, invoking the healing power of the Lord on the congregation so that it may move forward. By the same token, the praying interim can lead the officers of the church in being praying officers praying over the congregants with deep-seated emotions. This may include laying on of hands on a person in need, done either privately or publicly, depending on what the person needing healing finds important and comfortable. The interim may have to teach certain leaders to become the praying leaders they need to be. Of course, if a church has a prayer team, this should be invoked by the interim for the congregation during the duration the interim is on staff.

Comforting and Consoling

The interim further is a comforter and a consoler. Scripture calls the Holy Spirit the comforter. I am convinced that an interim is doing the work of the Holy Spirit and showing the presence of the Holy Spirit when comforting and consoling people in the church. The church needs someone to cry to. The church needs someone willing to accept its grief. The church needs someone upon whose shoulders it may lay its collective head and find consolation. This is where interims should shine.

Individually, an interim will hear the grief over the loss of a pastor. Individually, an interim will comfort and console people, assuring them that God is still with them and will help them. The interim will let the people know that by being present, they will see God's grace is real and continuing. God has put interim pastors in place physically so that the churches and individuals may experience physically the spiritual power and presence of God. In a very real way, interims at their best become the embodiment of Jesus Christ, who went around and healed, as Mark constantly reminds us.

It is always important that the interim be able to cite, use, direct, and provide Scriptures that are healing, comforting, consoling. Obviously, start with the Holy Spirit as comforter. Move on to Jesus healing. Consider many of the comforting Psalms. Pick up on the Beatitudes. Any good concordance will give you many Scriptural citations on healing, comfort, and consolation, among other synonyms. For that matter, these days many bibles have short concordances in the back or specific listings for certain concerns, including comforting and consoling. Anyone who has ever seen or been a recipient of a Gideon's Bible knows whereof I speak. Their bibles have intentionally added comforting listings and indeed listings for all types of needs that the reader can pick up and go right to. Additionally, many devotionals regularly focus on just such texts. Use these tools and make them available to those in the congregation who need them.

Healing Staff

An interim must be the pastor the church needs during the time the installed pastor is not yet in place or still just a dream. The interim will do all a pastor does, healing being essential. However, healing goes in many directions in a church without an installed pastor. There may need to be healing of the staff in light of the lack of installed pastors. Too many times I have walked into an interim position, only to find the hired staff (such as the secretary or the janitor or the church musicians or the youth director or the administrator or any of a number of other possibilities) lacking morale, drifting, anguished, upset, uncertain, and even lost. Sometimes the previous pastor was to blame; other times the staff has been fighting among themselves. At such times the staff clearly needs healing.

How do you heal the staff? It may be as simple as recognizing and thanking the staff. It may include having regular staff meetings so that staff can know what is going on and be included in the activities of the church. Such staff meetings also bring the staff together, and they learn to work together and hear each other. The interim may need to take the staff out for lunch occasionally or at least shortly after arriving. The interim should always pass on compliments heard about certain staff to the staff, and the interim should take time to compliment the staff for good work. Further, the interim should let the leaders of the church know the good works of the staff. Believe in the staff, and they will deliver. As Christians, we are supposed to be lifting each other up, supporting each other, and surely we can do that for staff.

Further, the interim should be available to the staff. This means helping the staff out. The interim is willing to help the secretary, the janitor, the Christian educator, the choir director, or whoever is on staff in ways that make it possible for the staff to do their jobs. The interim does not hide in the clergy's office, never to be seen by the staff. The interim spends time casually conversing with the staff, listening to them, learning from them, and taking seriously their thoughts and suggestions. Often, staff feel pastors do not take them seriously, and just to be taken seriously goes a long way to improve staff morale.

Gifts of Healing

If the interim has a sense of humor, that too can help. Jokes told in sermons can get people to laugh, chuckle, even smile. If there are jokes that can get people over their grief, all the better! There are so many joke books out there and online that even someone who is not a natural comedian can find appropriate humor to lighten people up. It has been said that humor is a sign of God because humor helps us to deal with things we could not face otherwise. When we can laugh, we can heal because the best humor deals with the issues that concern us. When we can laugh at those issues, we heal because we realize they can be laughed at and laughed away. Our issues are not the final word; the joy of the Lord is.

My daughter, besides being a pastor herself, is a trained vocalist. On her own once serving as a chaplain in a hospital, she sang to a dying patient and that patient's family. The patient found peace, and the family found healing. Why do I bring this up for an interim? Each interim has gifts that go beyond the usual. For some it may be music, and if so, that use of music used wisely can heal. We know for Alzheimer's patients that the last recognition to go is music, and thus such patients unable to be reached elsewise will respond to music. Hymns and familiar religious pieces of music can reach those patients who are church people. Music can heal. Music can touch souls in ways even the best preaching cannot. If the interim has the gift of music, it should be used for healing purposes.

Of course, there are other gifts for healing purposes. The arts—from writing to drawing to acting, among others—if used wisely in a hurting situation can heal. There are groups working with former military, putting them to work in disaster situations and finding that heals. Putting people to work in the church, finding a common physical task that needs the work of the congregation together, becomes a goal, and that heals a congregation. The wise and gifted interim can use any of these and other techniques to heal a congregation.

Something that speaks to the congregation and unifies the congregation in its work becomes a tool and a gift to the congregation. Interims need to continually look for something that speaks to the congregation, something that brings the congregation together, and something that so excites the congregation that by working together, the church finds healing.

Of course, it should be obvious that a pastor's preaching should include healing sermons. Whether using the lectionary, which does have a substantial number of comforting and healing texts, or the interim just spending time looking for powerful texts that provide assurance, hope, and comfort, the interim needs to preach healing. The congregation needs to hear, for example, Isaiah comforting the people, and the pastor talking about how the captivity of Israel can be helpful to a church that has faced difficulties and needs to know God is still with them as God was with Israel in captivity.

In Conclusion

I have waited until just now to say what should be clear and hopefully obvious. An interim has the freedom to heal that a regular pastor does not always have. The pastor cannot heal the anguish left behind after leaving a church, whether for good or for bad reasons. The pastor cannot heal issues, including staff and congregational members who may have had problems with the pastor. Even the most beloved of pastors and the most competent of clergy can only do so much. If there are bad aspects, the interim has extra work. The interim is there for the congregation for the duration and can deal with those issues and those people who need healing. The freedom to heal in short-term relationships is ideal for the church and wonderful for the subsequent pastor. Things change, and people see the change in the interim. It provides the freedom needed to heal. This is a gift and a goal of every good interim.

An interim pastor will find many opportunities to provide the healing of God the Father, God the Son, and God the Holy Spirit in the church setting. The interim who truly provides healing for the congregation in difficult times is a blessing to the church and truly serving our God. Such an interim is clearly needed when the church is without an installed pastor.

7

The Freedom to Explain

Communicate, communicate, communicate! If there is a motto for interim work, then "Communicate, communicate, communicate" is the phrase. It is absolutely essential that an interim communicates what is going on, why it is going on, what is the meaning of what is going on, how things will happen, and where does all of this lead to. The interim is there for a rather short time, and unless a church has had numerous interims, the church does not know what an interim is about. Sadly, even in churches that have had interims regularly, there is often a misunderstanding of the role of the interim.

The Bumpy, Curvy Road

The interim is leading a congregation through a process that leads to a new pastor. Typically, that process is bumpy and curvy, as bad as a rural mountain highway or as bad as an old farm road. We have all been on such highways, and unless we are a glutton for punishment, they are not our favorite highways. In the between time of an interim, the process causes massive grumbling, complaining, bitterness, and the oft-expressed desire to shorten and straighten out the process. Make this a straight short road, and we will be happy, say many parishioners.

For the sake of the congregation, it does not work that way. We have to put up with those bumpy, curvy roads to get to the other side, our destination. In the same way, we have to put up with the bumps and the curves in the process. The problems are real, and sometimes they guarantee a bumpy ride. Issues have to be dealt with, and some sneak up on us or are unexpected. Those are the curves that have to be straightened out, or at least handled properly in our driving hereafter, meaning living with the curves. Life is not easy, and interim work is not easy.

Everything

In short, the interim needs to explain everything or as close to everything as possible. I can hear readers ask sarcastically, "Everything?" Yes, I do mean everything. Explain the interim process. Explain what an interim can and cannot do. Explain what a church must do before it gets a new pastor. Explain why the interim is doing things differently than the previous pastor. Explain what you as an interim and an outsider see in the church and how that impacts the interim time in the church. Explain if you have the church or its leadership take surveys.

This is the freedom an interim has. I would love to say that every installed, regular, nontransitional pastor explained everything going on in the church. Unfortunately, I have not seen it. The good ones do, ordinarily. I say ordinarily because even the best ministers can become so busy as to really not have the time and cannot make the time to explain everything. Add in new members coming into the church, and I dare say those people will be in the dark about certain church things for some time. Hopefully, someone will get around to explaining what is obvious to veteran members, but it is unknown to a new member.

Treasurers and Finances

Typically, there are certain aspects of the church's life that are not explained, and usually for good reasons. Some of the church's work is highly technical, and it takes some effort to explain it. Try explaining the full report of the treasurer, especially if the treasurer is an accountant or has an accounting background. I have yet to serve in a church wherein the congregation could fully make sense of a treasurer's report. Too many times I have sat in board meetings and seen the bored eyes of the council as the treasurer goes over the financial report. Or worse, I have seen eyes glaze over because they did not know what the treasurer was even saying.

A good interim, indeed the best pastors, should be able to help the boards, councils, and appropriate committees make sense of financial reports. I am not saying the interim has to be an accountant, a bookkeeper, or some sort of financial whiz to be a good interim. Yet the interim can have the treasurer put the numbers into a format that the board members can appreciate or understand. Sometimes this involves more than numbers, like explaining in writing in simple English where such and such goes and why that figure is what it is.

The other side of a treasurer is too many of them are born pessimists or at least by nature highly negative. They assume the worst in their reports and often forget that by the end of the year, things improve. If the traditional history of the church supports that (and the interim should do that research), the interim will need to explain that in order to prevent the treasurer from leading the church astray financially.

Of course, there are times the church is in financial doo-doo, and that needs to be explained. Then the interim will have to lead the board to making the necessary cuts needed to ensure the solvency of the church. Indeed, if the church has been pretending it has money to do what it wants to do and it really does not, the interim has to explain the truth and work with the church to ensure it deals with the truth.

Membership

The truth shall set you free, says the Bible, and it is clearly shown when the interim becomes the truth teller to the congregation. The interim explains what is true and what is not true. Some churches unfortunately have not allowed themselves to face the truth about themselves. It can be as simple as not allowing the membership rolls actually to be honest. Too many churches have bloated membership numbers. The figures have no correlation to actual participation in the life of the church.

There are admittedly gray areas, as defining a member by who gives financially to the church, even if that person has not entered the church in years. They are still members that much, but have forgotten that money is not the only or even the major criterion for being a member. There is something about a visible presence in a church, and for that matter, a visible presence that actually participates in the life of the church. Some churches have tried to be totally honest and gone this way, and the actual numbers are then very smaller than when churches waffle on what makes an honest member of the congregation.

The gray area can be argued that even a gray presence or gray membership makes it possible for people to become more involved. Besides, we do not want to be in the business of throwing everybody out if they are not fully involved as only a few are. Who knows what seeds are being planted for gray members by allowing them to be gray members?

What I am saying is that both sides of the membership issue can be argued logically. The real question is whether or not the church is being honest about itself and how it understands membership. If it is a really committed membership church, then gray areas are excluded. If it is a church that hopes people will want to become more involved and is willing to accept people where they are even if they cannot leave the gray area, then the gray area is essential. Be honest about the church. An interim can explain the difference and help the congregation to be honest about itself and what that means to church membership.

When the Pastor Was Forced Out

If the previous pastor was forced out, has that been explained to the congregation? Has the congregation heard the truth about what happened or only rumors? Has the whole removal process been hush-hush, or was it dealt with openly and honestly? I have seen too many churches that believe the best way to handle such situations is, to use their words, be discreet. What they really mean is that they are not interested in telling the truth about what happened. They prefer to keep it buried, secretive, or at least minimally known. The congregation should not be burdened with the knowledge of what happened.

I reject such limitations. I reject such because I have seen what those limitations have done to churches and their membership. Let me give a few examples. A pastor engages in sexual hanky-panky with the organist, choir director, secretary, or some very prominent member of the church. The pastor is quickly shown the door, but the other participant is still present and active in the church. It takes two to tango, goes the old saying, but sometimes the church or those in authority don't believe that, or at least pretend not to believe it.

The organist, choir director, secretary, or other prominent member has allies in the church. The church leadership who removed the pastor or had the pastor removed by denominational types then hush up the full details to protect the other person. They really do not want to lose this other person, but rumors start to spread, and the rumors develop a life of their own. Often, the rumors are like the game where you whisper in someone's ear what you have been told in a whisper by the person sitting next to you. By the time the whispered lines get back to the original speaker, they are mangled, distorted, and very far from what the original whisperer said. Rumors have that type of life. One need only look at the Internet to see how rumors spread these days—maliciously, untruthfully, and way beyond what actually happened.

Eliminate, for another example, the stereotypical involvement of the pastor with a member in a sexual liaison. Staying with sexual themes though, what happens when a pastor is into pornography and uses the church computer for that purpose? Take that to the extreme and add in child pornography. Do churches talk honestly about such situations? Not from my point of view, not from what I have seen happen in a church thereafter. Of course, the pastor is ousted, but then too often, churches hush this up or, if all fails, try to manage the situation in such a way that it comes across as a sound bite you would hear from reporters or politicians. They are minimal assessments of what has actually happened, and as such are as confusing as they are limited in what they say or do not say.

Going to different type of categories, how does a church deal with a pastor who embezzles or a pastor who picks up a DUI conviction? Like the rest of humanity, there are pastors who have abused both legal and illegal drugs. There have been pastors who have taken financial advantage of elderly members. Sadly, there are any number of immoral actions pastors can do and, when caught, are removed from their positions.

The real question is whether or not the church will deal with those removals honestly or play games with them. I know that comes across as harsh. However, to the people in the pews who really do not know what is happening or why, or at best only hear rumors, the result is bad. They speculate badly. They judge badly. They look to blame badly. Too often, more than any of us like to admit, they will jump ship. I have heard people say they left a church because of how such situations were handled.

The truth may be ugly, but it is the truth. If people really do not want to hear the truth, that is their choice. It is not, however, the choice of those who removed a person from the pastoral position. If someone comes up to the group or individual involved in removing the previous pastor and asks why, that person (or those persons) needs to be prepared to give a clear explanation why, with illustrations if necessary. If a pastor is being removed, the people involved in the removal process have to be able to explain the reasons to anyone who asks. They did it; they need to justify what they did. Often in such situations, the interim will either have to coach the people in what to say or just be the person who can clearly say what happened and why. After all, some people have a hard time communicating, and they may well need training to explain. In worst cases, they may need a substitute to explain what they cannot properly explain.

Any lawyer knows there are witnesses, and there are witnesses. Some are very good; some are very bad. Plus, there are witnesses in between. Consider that a parallel to what church members face when a pastor is forced out. Even those who have witnessed and been involved in the situation may not be the best witnesses when it comes to explaining what happened and why. The interim works with people as lawyers work with witnesses to prepare them to be the best they can be. When the witness is unable to witness, the lawyer excludes that witness from testifying and finds alternatives to ensure the story is told.

It is the same way with churches dealing with pastors forced out. The interim learns what the witness can say, does know, and is able to repeat. The interim listens to as many of these witnesses as possible, and then puts together a coherent understanding of what happened and why. The interim may be thereafter the one to share this, or the interim may find special persons within the congregation able to share this. The fact is the information will be shared clearly and logically.

Admittedly, there will be emotions involved in removing a pastor and how people feel about the removal after the fact, but the interim will work to ensure the story is presented as logically and clearly as possible. The emotions will be kept to a minimum in telling the story, unless they are essential to the story. Some pastors leave behind emotional wrecks, and if that is the case, that must be included in the story. If it is criminal or immoral behavior involved, that can be presented without the accompanying emotions. In either case, communicate, explain, present the story.

Do not hide the facts. Do not allow the facts to be excluded Do not pretend that everything is hunky-dory once the pastor is gone. That is just the beginning. You have to deal with people in the congregation before the healing can begin. You have to let people hear what happened in order for them to make sense of it and move on. Be prepared for questions. Be prepared to prove your case. Also, be sensitive to those for whom the dismissed pastor made a real difference.

Let's be honest. Even crooks can do good things. Even the worst of pastors can make a difference for some people. Be very aware that these people who have experienced the best from a bad pastor will be hurting because that pastor was important to them. While you will need to explain what happened and why to them, you will also need to deal with them pastorally. This means being gentle with their feelings. You will have to hear their good reports about the bad pastor and accept the good the bad pastor did.

Indeed, for those clearly involved in the removal of the bad pastor, they will have to be informed of the good such a bad pastor did. The bad clearly overwhelms the good, but the good must be acknowledged and allowed to be heard. It is easy to judge people absolutely as good or bad. The Bible itself does this with many of the kings of Israel and Judah. Check out First and Second Kings and First and Second Chronicles to see how this plays out. Yet in many cases, people are not absolutely good or bad; they are clearly bad or clearly good. However, they have both bad and good in them. A bad pastor who needed to be removed did some good, and that needs to be acknowledged and appreciated, as uncomfortable as it may be for those who removed such a person.

Remember, even bad pastors are not always demonic, and to demonize someone, even a bad pastor, leads churches down very dangerous territory. Such demonizing can come back to cause problems for the church. Get your facts straight and tell the story the way it needs to be told, realizing we are all human, and there but for the grace of God go I.

Pastor Killers

Now I need to deal with the other side of removing a pastor—where the pastor removed should not have been removed. At the most extreme are churches that are pastor killers. Other churches allow certain people in the church to bully the congregation and remove any pastor who does not fully allow the bully to bully. There are also churches that have unreasonable expectations for pastors, and when inevitably a pastor does not live up to those expectations, the pastor is removed. I have actually seen churches put on their official résumés they are looking for a pastor who can walk on water. I hope they are joking, but in light of pastors being removed for unreasonable expectations, I am not so convinced. No pastor can do everything, but too many churches think the pastor should. When the pastor is shown to be human, that is too much for the churches, and they remove the pastor.

Interims put into such situations have to explain to the congregation what they have done. Interims will have to clearly let the congregation know of their bad patterns. Interims in such situations may well have to name names. They will clearly have to show why such behavior leads churches astray and assures that pastors will not stay. Interims in such positions have to lead the congregation to better behaviors, clearer understandings, reducing expectations, and dealing with the problems in their own churches. The interim will have to go into great detail about why this is necessary. It may well include going over the history of the church and pointing out the historical patterns. It may well mean saying such and such is controlling you. Is that what you really want, or do you want to be a church where clergy can function?

Discipline

Most churches have disciplinary actions able to be used on members who are disciplinary problems. I would suggest interims know these materials intimately and be prepared to bring them to the attention of those in authority. One would hope they are used sparingly, but they are available because they are needed. Use them when there are people who cannot be reached any other way.

The interim may have to talk to the tough people in the congregation. The interim may have to try to reason with such people. The interim who does this should never go alone, but always have someone or several someones there who can attest to what happened in such meetings. Unfortunately, people being controlling people will always try to manipulate or deceive or even lie about what they have been told. When confronted with more than one person, their manipulations, deceptions, and lies are exposed as to what they are.

Eventually, the interim will have to lead the people into standing up to those causing problems in the church. Those types of people have to be shown how their behavior is causing problems, and those willing to stand up to such people have to be willing to say what needs to be said to such people. The interim will need to coach the people into being willing to fight the bad influences. The interim will need to explain to the people willing to stand up why they are essential and how they can do what needs to be done. It may well take some training time. It may well take providing very specific teachings to those who can and will act on how to do so effectively.

Whatever it takes to bring a bad church out of the dark into the light, the interim will need to clarify, explain, and communicate to the congregation. No doubt some of this information shared will be received unhappily, even negatively. Some people may become obstructionist. The information must be shared openly, and people must be made aware of what needs to be done to change the church's atmosphere. What is poisoned must be removed. What is toxic must be cleansed. What is polluted must be cleaned up. Whatever is causing the church to fail its pastors must be brought to everyone's attention and then dealt with.

The Forum

An interim needs to be able to use various communication tools. One tool I have found particularly helpful and effective is the forum. A forum, as I have used it, begins with an open invitation to the congregation to hold open a certain date and a certain time to meet together to discuss openly what the church is about and where the church is going. Unless a church has success at bringing people together other than on Sundays, I suggest it be done on Sundays, most commonly after worship (the last worship if there is more than one service). I believe the people should be fed at such an event, as people are more likely to attend if fed. Food is provided by a caterer so that everyone attending can be involved instead of being forced to handle the food issues.

Once the meal is done, divide people up so that a variety of people sit at each table (counting off, numbers on tags, or any of a number of ways to randomize who is sitting with whom). Give each table prepared questions they have not seen before dealing with matters in the church, but also have one open-ended question so that nothing is overlooked. Each person at the table has to answer each of the questions first in writing then openly with the others at the table. No one can interrupt each person's presentation. Someone acts as a secretary for each table to report on what each person says. The overall reports are picked up and kept by the church as it considers what those in the church feel are important.

If done properly, it can have people listening to each other; issues will be raised the body can generally agree upon. It will make communication possible and allow all people to be heard and provide the opportunity for people to say what has not been said. It is a tool, but there are other tools. Look at how the church communicates with each other. Use those that work to communicate carefully, thoughtfully, and fully.

Whatever Works

Whether from the church pulpit, newsletters, social media, special correspondences, congregational meetings, informal gatherings, church-provided meals, through certain people, or any of number of other possibilities, find what works best to communicate accurately and honestly all that needs to be communicated. Use them. An interim should dig them out and find what works best and then use them regularly, constantly, repeatedly.

Some churches communicate well through their committees. Therefore, the committees themselves can become a tool for communication. If necessary, a separate committee can be established for communication purposes. Whatever it is called, it meets to understand what needs to be communicated to the congregation, and then it does so. Sometimes such a committee may be a task force or other grouping organized to evaluate what is needed in the congregation and then work to implement those needs, communicating constantly about why these needs must be met.

In Conclusion

Whenever there is a question, explain. Whenever uncertainty hovers around issues, explain. Whenever someone is just not getting it, explain. Whenever people complain about the pace of things, explain. Whenever something significant happens, explain. Whenever decisions must be made, explain. It is better to explain too much, and people will generally tell you when they receive enough information. Yet always be prepared to explain anything and everything. You may have to do so.

This is the freedom the interim has. The interim is there to ensure a church moves on. If a church is enmeshed in confusion, miscommunication, deception, lies, fears, misunderstandings, half truths, and doubts, there is no possibility of that happening. The interim must ensure the communication makes it possible for a church to hear, to understand, to accept, and ultimately to trust in God's workings in Jesus Christ by the Holy Spirit through the church in this interim period.

Explanation comes out of communication, and the communication the interim models makes it possible for the church to be the church. Yes, the truth will set you free. Consequently, explain the truth in love. The truth must be heard, must be explained, and must be understood. It is not easy, but it is necessary for the church. The interim has the freedom to explain like nobody else in the church, and it is absolutely essential the interim use this freedom.

8

The Freedom to Terminate

When I was in training to be an interim minister with other interims, we were asked to do a case study of the church we were serving, something significant in the life of the church. I decided on the fact the church wanted me to get rid of the church choir director. The church leadership did not have the gumption to do that, though they knew it was necessary. I was given the task of making that happen. I brought this information to the teachers and learned, to my dismay, that I would be the very first person to present a case study. When I asked why, I was told that often the interim gets stuck with terminating staff or people the church knows it needs to get rid of, but the previous pastor could not and the church itself cannot. The interim gets the job.

Whoopee! Let's face it. Nobody really likes to fire people, and especially we Christian folk will seek any excuse not to fire someone. We really do not want to cause pain, we say. We don't want to hurt someone's feelings, we say. The person is important to the church, and we can't afford to lose this person, we say. There are all sorts of excuses and rationalizations for not firing people who need to be fired.

Undesirable Staff

However, if the organist is totally incompetent, the person has to be let go. If the secretary cannot do the work, the secretary has to be removed. If technology has changed and the person handling the technology is unwilling or unable to learn the latest, such a person needs to be replaced. A janitor may be dictating to the congregation when the church may be used or the cleaning schedule at his or her convenience instead of when the church really is needed. A choir director may become so abusive to the choir members that they are quitting in droves. There are all sorts of reasons for terminating staff—from the criminal to the ineffective to the tail-wagging-the-dog syndrome.

Yes, as I pointed out about the janitor in my hypothetical above, the janitor may dictate to the church, and the church is then at the mercy of the janitor. The janitor is paid staff to do the work of the church and is under the direction of the church, not vice versa. When the janitor dictates to the church, it is a case of the tail wagging the dog, instead of the dog wagging the tail.

I have seen too many instances of staff dictating to the church, and the church lets the staff get away with it. Staff are working for the church; the church is not working for the staff. An interim appears on the scene, and lo and behold, the interim gets the job of doing what nobody else will do: eliminate the bad staff. After all, the interim is temporary and can be blamed by the congregation or anybody else for the fact. Use the interim to do what everybody knows is necessary, and then blame the interim or use the interim as a scapegoat for any repercussions that follow.

Welcome to the world of the interim. The interim has the incredible freedom to terminate, fire, remove, eliminate, or get rid of undesirable staff, and for good measure, bad elements in the church. Let's face a painful truth. While there are clergy and churches willing to terminate people, they do not like to do it and try to avoid it at all costs. If push comes to shove, like something genuinely criminal (for example, embezzlement by the treasurer), usually such a person will be terminated promptly. However, there are exceptions I know about. I have regularly heard about embezzlers being forgiven by the church and left in their positions. Sometimes they change, but often they do not, and the church eventually has to act.

Pastors are human beings with feelings who take their Christianity seriously. They want to forgive everyone, but forget that forgiveness implies repentance when someone does something wrong. A person who will not change for the better is a problem to a church and to clergy who simply cannot understand such people. There are evil people in this world. There are incompetent people in this world. There are people who misuse positions of authority in this world. There are people who really think the world revolves around them. There are people who, put in a job, ignore everyone else and want the job defined to suit them as they define it. They really do not care about rules, regulations, church needs, or anything other than what they want to do when they want to do it. Sometimes their actions lead to crimes; often it leads to irreconcilable conflicts with other staff and the church.

An interim with a track record of dealing with people who need to be terminated will get churches precisely needing such skills. I confess to being such an interim. I have regularly dealt with staff that were incompetent and needed to be removed but were not by the previous pastor or by the church itself. The interim got the job. I got the job. I had to find a way to remove the person from the position. This direction was given to me with one caveat: do it with Christian love.

Helping People to Resign

Try telling a person he or she is fired with Christian love. It does not happen. Instead, I have found it better and more easily absorbed if the person can be helped to see the necessity for resigning. Such a person needs to develop a mind-set that allows for the possibility of withdrawing from a position. I work with people so that they can see the need in and of themselves. Often, these people have a feeling it is time to step down, and they only need support and acceptance of them, indeed affirming them as people and as following the will of God to step down.

In other words, I work with such people in a gentle, affirming, but strong way. I want them to own the possibility and not see it as in any way a condemnation of them. I will talk to them about how they see the position and what it means to the church and to them. Of course, before leading people to removal, I try to work with them and help them, where possible, to improve. As a result, there have been people I have saved from the execution block. However, when

I am called to terminate someone, it is pretty clear such people need to be terminated.

I am saying that the business model of kicking someone out in a cold, insensitive, "protect the business over the person" manner is not the pattern for the church. One does not evade the responsibility, the necessity, the genuine need to remove such people. We have all heard about churches that let sexually abusive people not face the consequences of their actions because we really can change such people. In all honesty, I doubt it. Only when such a person accepts responsibility for their actions and realizes how wrong it was will there be change. Alcoholics Anonymous is absolutely right about that.

Due Process

Yet if the church is to stand for its faith, there is such a thing as compassion when removing people from positions of authority. I admit and accept that in dangerous situations, the person has to be removed immediately, automatically, and completely. These situations are pretty obvious: sexual misconduct, murderous intents or actions, suicidal or other mentally dangerous situations (a person loses all sense of reality, for example), among others. In those circumstances, a person cannot be allowed to continue.

My only caveat is to be willing to provide due process to such a person. I have known of sexual offenders who should never have been in the ministry, but they were. I have seen pastors lose it mentally, and they needed to be in treatment. I have even heard of cases where a pastor allowed anger to be so controlling that despite the Christian background, murder was contemplated or actually instituted. Having said that, I have also known cases where evil people falsely accuse the pastor of something heinous in order to get rid of the pastor or to cover up something in their own lives. Be sure of the facts. Yes, suspend or remove them, but if the facts do not hold up, be prepared to deal with that reality in a Christian way. Also, if the facts are false, be prepared to deal with the false accuser so that he or she will not do this again.

Troublemakers

This caveat also goes for the people in the church. There are people in the church who are bad, and there are people in the church

around whom false rumors and accusations are common. Be sure of the facts. Be prepared to deal with false accusers. Terminating false accusers in a church is often as necessary as terminating problem staff.

In the best cases, terminating false accusers happens automatically. The person realizes the lie has been exposed, and the person voluntarily withdraws. Actually, I have seen this happen a good number of times. When the truth comes to light, people who are afraid of the light run away. I would love to say that people will repent and realize the error of their ways. Some do, no doubt, thank God. Unfortunately, a person whose church career has been a matter of lies and deceptions finds it hard to give up on those lies and deceptions. Such a person usually finds it easier to leave the church rather than face up to the consequences of the lies and deceptions.

For the sake of the church, not only staff but also members of the church have to be terminated from the church. At the least if it is possible, the person should be terminated from certain responsibilities in the church. If a person is causing problems with a church fund-raiser, that person should be prevented from having anything to do with that fund-raiser. If a person is attacking staff falsely, that person should be prevented from having anything to do with the staff. If a person is serving on the official board of the church and is nothing but a troublemaker on the board, that person should be removed from the board and prevented from serving on that board again.

Unfortunately, these types of termination are never easy. Occasionally, I have found people who simply accept the fact they are causing problems and realize they need to step down from the position of authority. More typically, these are people who do not see themselves as a problem while everyone else does. They need to be confronted by the truth, usually with several people in attendance and witnessing to the fact. Sometimes this works; it should at least be tried. The Bible itself reminds us to go to a Christian one-on-one and then with others, and if that does not work, to treat them as outsiders.

There are people who misuse the church and will not listen to reason, no matter what. Every pastor can tell stories about people who jump from church to church, stirring up trouble in each church they attend. They want the church on their own terms and under their own rule instead of how God wants the church. These are people who really are not ready for church leadership and must be kept out of such positions. If they get in such positions, they need to be removed as fast as possible. The interim may have to force such a person out, making it so uncomfortable for that person in that position that the person will resign. If this does not work, others need to be present at a specially called meeting with the person and be forcefully honest and insist on that person withdrawing. Ultimately, if that fails, have the official board sanction such a person and forbid that person from serving further.

I realize this comes close to that dangerous and scary word, *excommunication*, or to a lesser degree, that word used in other religious circles: *shunning*. The idea behind both concepts is to lead persons to repentance, not throw them away and give up on them. We want to develop loving, good, caring Christians, not people for whom Christianity is a weapon to be used against anyone who gets in our way. Some people live for power, and the Lord's Prayer reminds us that power ultimately belongs to God alone. When we are given power, it is always to be used under God's guidance for good—not for evil, not for self, and not for anything that demonizes the church. Thus, it is necessary to do what is needed to remove, terminate, and otherwise prevent such people from using positions in the church for wrong purposes.

Prevention

The reader may have recognized that I use the word *terminate* in a very broad sense. One concept included is prevention. There are people who need to be prevented from causing problems; they must, in effect, be terminated from ever being put into such positions to cause problems. Let us face it, we all know people in churches who should never serve in positions of authority. If they get on, they are disasters an interim will have to find a way to remove. Ideally, the interim and others in the church will realize this and prevent such people from ever having that authority.

Many churches have nominating processes to put people on boards. Use those processes to prevent a bad person from getting on the board. Preventing disasters are easier than dealing with disasters. The interim usually gets both, but an astute interim will find means to ensure a disaster does not happen, and that means by not giving a disastrous person a tool to be disastrous. The church has enough problems without adding one more.

We may want to be nice to such a person. We may want to include such a person. We may feel such a person will change in positions of authority. We may feel it is the Christian thing to do. I am saying such feelings are not good for the church. As the old cliché goes, an ounce of prevention is worth a pound of cure. It is always easier to prevent a problem than to cure a problem. Doctors and the insurance industry know this well, which is why they encourage prevention.

The Interim as Politician

This is one of those clear cases an interim needs to be a good politician. The politicians who succeed are those who know how to work within the system without hurting people in the process. They are not cutthroat, but rather creative in dealing with people. Thus, even if people disagree with the politician, they still respect the person and acknowledge the person's worth and value. This is an earned trust because the successful politician is not out to destroy people but instead to convert people or work with people in all situations.

Therefore, the interim needs to know how to work within the system, even at times controlling the system, in other words use it politically in order to prevent disasters from happening. I wish I could say that pastors are adept at this skill. I have seen those who are, but I have also seen those who are not. Some ministers find politics dirty and will not "condescend" to that level. This is another case of misunderstanding politics and its values. Politics is a tool for better or for worse. Some use it badly and give politics a bad name. Others use it well, and we honor such leaders with terms like *statesman, honorable, well-loved, respected*, and the like.

If we remind ourselves that everything is political, we might be willing to work politically but in a Christian way. There is a bureaucracy in place in the church, which can be used to prevent disasters from happening. A bureaucracy that takes its political tasks seriously is a bureaucracy that prevents disasters from happening.

In Conclusion

The freedom to terminate has become an assumed, typical, expected task for the interim pastor. Therefore, the interim has to be prepared to deal with it. I do agree with the interim teachers I had; it is almost normal for an interim. Where the pastor could not act, the interim can. The freedom to terminate is a serious freedom, one not to be taken lightly, but it is absolutely essential for an interim. If the interim does not act to terminate when termination is necessary, the church will have problems thereafter. Sadly, I have seen new pastorates badly damaged, if not destroyed, because the interim did not terminate someone who needed to be terminated.

Therefore, when the interim sees people that need to be terminated or is asked by the official body to terminate someone, do so. It is a freedom given to the interim specifically and must be used accordingly. The interim can do it; that is one aspect of being an interim. The freedom to terminate is accordingly a gift the interim is blessed to invoke. Used in proper and helpful ways, the interim's freedom to terminate makes it possible for the church to be the church of Jesus Christ.

9

The Freedom to Change

The freedom to change is the most basic freedom an interim has. Anytime an interim is brought onto the scene, everyone assumes that minister is there to bring change. In every previous chapter, changes have been given for each topic. Whether it is change in staff (the freedom to terminate), change in discussing matters openly (the freedom to communicate), change in the pain people feel (the freedom to heal), change in administration (the freedom to override or veto), change in attitude (the freedom to disagree), change in how things get done (the freedom to act), change in worship (the freedom of worship), and change in how people talk (freedom of speech), changes accompany each and every freedom an interim has.

Yet there is more to change an interim brings than was given in previous chapters. The most obvious is the presence of the interim per se. This is a change from a permanent, installed, regular pastor. This person is temporary, and that is a change. It means this person is only here for a relatively short time and then is gone. Thus, the congregation has to get used to the fact that there was a change from the previous pastor, and there will again be a change to the new pastor, all within a short time period. The sheer presence of an interim is a living embodiment of change.

The Gold Standard

In every church I have served, whether as the permanent or the temporary pastor, inevitably someone (or more likely several or more people) brings up a past minister who was golden. By this I mean the pastor was beloved, and the time that pastor served were golden days for the church. Every new pastor, whether permanent or temporary, has to face up to the golden pastor because every pastor is judged by the golden standard.

"You are not like Pastor…" "Oh, you don't even look or dress like Pastor…" "Pastor…had such a way." "The church has not been the same since Pastor…" Substitute the proper title for each church (father, reverend, doctor, etc.), and the effect is still the same. No two people are exactly the same, and the gold standard puts many ministers at an automatic disadvantage. Especially tricky is when an interim comes right in after the golden clergy because just that presence indicates a guaranteed change from the golden one.

It is no good to try to knock down the golden standard. That is a recipe for disaster because the golden time was indeed a good time. It makes any successor look mean-spirited and petty, and such a person is insecure and willing to be nasty to uplift their own ministry. Paul, when faced with others' work at Corinth, for example, uplifted their work, supported their work, and pointed out they were all in this together. We are all in the ministry, whenever and wherever we serve. Blessed be those who have served in the past and served well! That is the only appropriate response.

A different person is going to be different. Times change. People are not the same. Ministry means different things at different times. Any minister needs to build on the work of others, support the work of others, and then move on to the future, which inevitably means changes. The interim's presence helps the congregation to see that whoever comes next is not going to be the same as whoever was there before. The future is laid out ahead, and it can never be exactly the same as the past. That is the way it is with a different pastor, and that is the way it will be with the church.

An interim who is there for more than just one day of worship or a few weeks of worship but is rather there for perhaps a year or more just by being there physically gets across to the congregation this is a time of change. The next pastor will be different. The next clergy will not be the same. The church will not be the same.

Overcoming Fear of Change

Once that realization sinks in, the immediate response is fear of change. On a very intellectual level, the congregation realizes the need for change, but on a visceral, emotional, and very basic gut level, fear of change is central. Look at how technology has changed us in the last twenty years. Think of something you did not have twenty years ago and what you consider as basic and necessary now. Consider also certain technologies that scared you or you still do not use, though many others do.

Alvin Toffler talked about "future shock," and it is even more prevalent now than when he wrote his book. Future shock is just another way to say fear of change. Change is fearful. Change is frightening. Change is scary. Indeed, looking at the past history of the twentieth century would give anyone living through that time a genuine fear. For that matter, anyone looking back and expecting that history repeats itself or at least somewhat copies itself has to be uneasy, even fearful about the future.

Therefore, change in a church too is fearful. After all, many people come to church to find a bearing, a stability, a base in a world of constant, even terrible changes. To discover that the church changes too can be disconcerting, at the least. I would suggest therefore that the church can model change to a fearful world. An interim can lead the people to see the good, the hopeful, the best in change. Indeed, they can begin to see God at work in change, leading ultimately to the kingdom of God on earth. They begin to realize that God works in the world, even when evil is at its worst. They begin to see how God can work in all times to bring about the promised new heaven and new earth. They realize that Jesus is Lord and he went to the cross, the ultimate evil, to bring life, forgiveness, grace, love, and eternity to all who believe. Further, Jesus died on that cross to overcome the forces of evil that seek to prevent the kingdom of heaven from coming on earth. We pray, "Thy kingdom come, on earth, as it is in heaven." That is as basic a theological underpinning for change as there can be.

We know the earth now is not as it is in heaven. We want that to happen. We pray, "Lord, come." We seek the return of the Lord.

We seek the peaceable kingdom on earth that Scripture promises. We seek the end of disease, disaster, and ultimately death that are guaranteed in our faith. Therefore, we need change, God-given, God-led, God-assured change in Jesus Christ by the power and presence of the Holy Spirit.

An interim can preach that. An interim can show that. An interim can push for that. An interim can thereby show that change is the Lord's work and thus good work. A church needs to change to meet the Lord. A church needs to change for the sake of the Lord. A church needs to change in the times to work for the Lord. Interims succeed in the Lord when they help a church to realize the gift of change in the Lord. Getting people beyond the fear of change to realizing change is a gift of the Lord is a holy charge for the interim.

Whether it is getting the church to see needs in the community that are unmet and having the church respond, or upgrading the physical facility of the church that has been long needed, an interim should clearly take the point for change. Look for activities, events, commitments, missions, and groupings to change. It may mean starting up activities. Thus, as examples (and each church has to make its own decisions in light of what it is as a church), a church under an interim may decide to deal with the homeless by making its facilities available or by providing meals to them. The church because of its location may discover it can be instrumental in supporting the community and various organizations within the community. Sometimes just having a church find a new mission activity and then get enthusiastic about it can so make a difference in the life of the church that the congregation cannot stop talking about it. Maybe a church simply becomes enthusiastic about evangelism and, as a result, starts to bring people into the midst. Enthusiasm is always good for a church, and an interim should be the cheerleader invoking that enthusiasm from the members.

Physical Changes

I have been surprised how many times on the other side of having a church that physical needs have not been met for years. Thus, the appropriate building and grounds committee has to be led to do the work that needs to be done. The furnace is causing issues. The roof is leaking. Certain windows are cracked. The parking lot is in disrepair. The carpeting is ragged. Chairs and tables are worn out. The list is as endless as the building in which the church is located.

Some churches are very good at maintaining their facilities, but others allow repairs to drift. The installed pastor may not have had the energy to push through a major capital repair program with all the funding costs that involve. Or even if the money was available, the time and effort to ensure the work is done is daunting. One of my common tasks in all my aspects of ministry has been getting churches to do physical work on their facility they have neglected, overlooked, postponed, or otherwise did not get around to doing.

It may just be a push to the appropriate groups and ensuring the work gets done by being point for the work. It may involve raising the issue with influential people and letting a groundswell develop to deal with it. It may mean having people in the congregation see the issues up front and then acting upon it. It may mean just taking the bull by its horns and insisting upon it. Of course, it helps if some higher level of the denomination of which you are a part insists that certain work must be done before a new pastor is called. The interim may need to point this out to the official denominational types who would definitely want this to be handled and would point this out to the congregation.

Using Talents for Change

Of course, if the interim is a teacher, a new Bible study or contemporary issues study or some other type of study that would be a change for the church could be instituted. If the interim has theatrical skills, they could be used in ways the congregation has not previously experienced (whether in using them in preaching or providing genuine theatrical experiences). The interim has talents that can be used. If the interim is talented musically, find ways to use those musical skills in new possibilities for the church. An interim should not hide talents but use them, exploit them, make them come alive for the sake of the congregation. Who knows? God may have put you in such a place at such a time for such a reason (if I may paraphrase Esther). An interim is different and has talents. Let the congregation see them.

On a personal note, I play around with puppets. I am not a trained ventriloquist, nor would I qualify as a professional puppeteer. However, I do buy and use hand puppets that are child-friendly. Often, Vacation Bible Schools have puppets as an optional part of their programs. I buy these and use them. I have no problem playing a role with the puppets, whether the kids see me or not as I perform with them. I cannot tell how many times children have come up to me later and told me how much the puppets meant to them. For good measure, after I leave a church, I have heard from the children and their parents about how they enjoyed my doing what I did with the puppets.

All I am saying is that everyone has talents. Allow the church to see and experience what is different to them by using your talents. Doing so provides a good change and helps the congregation to see how good change can be.

Changing the Atmosphere of a Church

The hardest part of change for an interim is to change the atmosphere of a church if it is basically toxic. The interim has the freedom to act on such changes because that is basic to an interim. Whether it is the structure that has to be revised or the people's attitude that needs to be adjusted, the interim as an agent for change has to hit the floor running. The time is limited, and it is essential the interim act to ensure the church is a holy place instead of a toxic place.

The interim will quickly discover (unless previously advised by others in the know) where changes have to be made and have to be made fast. This may involve talking to people in the church to discover what is what and where the bad is festering. It helps when others outside of the church are in the know (like denominational and neighboring types) and can point the interim in the right direction to make changes. However, there are times when the interim has to uncover the problem areas without any previous knowledge and then act.

The point is to get to those problem areas and change them specifically. If one of the boards or councils is problematic, be prepared to change it. If people are creating an atmosphere that is unholy, be prepared to change them. If the organization of the church is dangerous, be prepared to reorganize and thus change it. If the personnel of the church are a hazard, be prepared to confront and if necessary remove them, thus changing them.

It may be necessary to revise personnel policies. It may be essential to change committees. It may be important to establish a new procedure manual. It may be crucial to have different people in charge of major tasks in the church. Sometimes, the same people in the same positions for many years can create a stagnation that must be broken and changed by having others take over their positions. Seek out, discover, nurture, and train new people who are committed to changing the church for the better. They will be the leaders, the core, the essentials needed to ensure what is wilted will be blooming again. They will find from the interim the strength and the passion to bring about needed change. They will lead the way, if the interim finds and supports them.

When Not to Change

Obviously, not all change will be good for a church. Change just to change is not helpful. Change must be brought about because there are reasons for change. If an interim changes something just because the interim does not like it, even though it is working well, at that point the interim is imposing a viewpoint on a church instead of serving the church. As I have said before, biases, ideologies, or agendas imposed on a church because the interim is obsessed with those perspectives have no place in solid interim work. The interim is to work within the system. The interim is to respect the church. The interim is to help the church be the best at what it is best at. Where there is no need for change, no change should be instituted.

Where Change Is Needed

Where there is a demonstrated need for change, change must be instituted. Some changes will be simple—somebody new doing a routine task, for example, because the previous doer is no longer able to do so. Other changes are very complex; undertaking a wholesale revision of the system of operating the church because the present system is totally dysfunctional takes sophistication and care. Most changes are in the middle range, not simple but not complex either. Changing the way the congregation actually brings people into leadership positions because the present way is not working and not bringing new people along takes an awareness of what will work under the circumstances and what will not. It may mean individually finding people and then bringing them to the attention of those who can ensure they are included in positions of leadership. Or if the present leadership is so entrenched, it may involve the church equivalent of guerrilla warfare. Take jabs here and there at weak places, soft places, places that the present leadership cannot fully control and put new people there. By doing so, you have started to provide an alternative leadership crew who can be seen and appreciated for their work by the congregation. Eventually, people in the congregation will insist these new leaders be given fuller and more responsible positions. When the demand becomes strong enough, the entrenched leadership will have no choice but to allow these "newbies" into the functioning of the church. At that point, they can bring about the changes that can only come through leadership positions.

I have not even touched on changes with basic tools or the essentials of the church. Hymnals wear out, or they are so outdated that the church is making its own supplements. Admittedly, dealing with changing hymnals is not an easy task as people become invested in hymnals. Yet there comes a time and a place for changing hymnals, which may also include how the music is presented. Even if the church keeps hymnals, newer ones are needed to help the church be the church of the times again and not a church stuck in a long-gone time period. To change hymnals often requires people willing to go all out to ensure change can happen. They point out the condition of the hymnals. They point out some new hymns that people are hearing elsewhere. They find the money needed, ideally from trusts or special accounts, but also from people who are willing to contribute financially in order to ensure new hymnals are purchased. It is a campaign, and it takes times to change hymnals, but those who see the need can make it happen if done graciously and like a campaign, pushing until the campaign is successful.

The same can happen with bibles, Sunday school materials, curricula, church artwork, toys, nursery supplies, and indeed many old and outdated resources sitting around the church. It may be necessary to have a clean-up day in which stuff sitting around forever is finally disposed of. Every church I have been associated with has a bad habit of hoarding stuff that should have been chucked years ago. Once you have a clean-up day, it becomes a start to help churches get beyond holding on to stuff just because this is the church to seeing that the church needs to be up-to-date and relevant for the times. Thus, the church will invest in new technology, will go for new materials, will find better equipment for the children, will do what it takes to make the church present itself in an appealing, updated light in which people will enjoy exploring what is new in the life of the church. That is a good change, a worthy change, a change necessary to bring the church up to the times and be a place that people want to attend.

In Conclusion

The goals of change in the church are twofold: bringing a church up to the times and ensuring the church is a place people want to attend. Making those points clear to the congregation, communicating them clearly to the congregation, and ensuring they are central to the changes being made will provide the atmosphere needed to bring about change in the church. People want to know why change is necessary, what that change means, and how that change can help the congregation. An interim working to bring a church up to the times and ensuring the church is a place where people will attend will find an eager audience, an enthusiastic audience, and especially a working audience, meaning an audience willing to work to bring about the changes needed.

The interim has the freedom to change because that is what an interim does, that is what an interim means, and that is why churches call interims in the first place. Used wisely and well, the freedom to change will bring a church up to the times and ensure the church is a place where people will attend.

10

The Freedom to Experiment

Churches like any group can get into a rut. The church does not seem to have its pizzazz, its mojo, its jive, or whatever else you want to call its excitement, its ability to shine and stand out as a church, and what has made it a unique and special church. Something is not quite there and maybe has not been there for some time. No one quite knows how to define it or even to say with certainty what is needed to ensure its return or at least provide a new start or some sort of revitalization.

In such cases, experimentation is needed. The interim has a great freedom to experiment that usually the regular pastor does not. Often the continuity is needed over a reconsideration of the whole church. The value of the interim is the ability to offer a period of renewal, reconsideration, and revitalization. To do so means the willingness to experiment.

Start Simple

How so? Start simple and in light of what people already know and understand. Thus, perhaps a new Bible study or topical study that covers something not previously (or perhaps many years ago prior to most of the congregation's memory) studied. Maybe it will include, especially if it is topical, something controversial that will get people talking and want to be involved. What does the church think of this issue? What do Christians think of such an issue? What do you as people of this church think of this issue? It may require a lot of discussion time as well as inviting experts in the field to come to the class or some church-wide event on the issue. Find something biblical or topical that catches people's attention, and to quote a popular movie, "They will come."

Food

Another place to experiment is by providing new fellowship groups, especially if the church is lacking in ongoing fellowship groups. These groups should have food, whether by the group itself or catered. Food is essential to the lifeblood of the church, and we fellowship best around food. Each church has to decide what type of fellowship-with-food groups are attractive to people. What will bring people out? What will get people to put aside their schedules and attend these groups? One way is to have these as a combination of devotion (short) followed by a time to get to know each other better and talk to each other. There may be formal topics of discussion, or there may be times of prayer or even occasions for people to talk about their concerns.

These types of groups can be as casual or as formal as the church finds people willing to come. Some churches have rediscovered the English high tea, where people just drink tea, eat snacks, and visit socially in the Lord. Of course, you can substitute coffee for tea or even water. You could have people make special desserts or, in good English tradition, homemade breads.

Is there a functioning men's group in the church, and do they meet for meals (often breakfasts, but lunch works as well, especially if the men work)? Do the women's groups eat together socially? Are there intergenerational meals? Is there an ongoing senior's group eating together? Are there groups that combine new members with veteran members and allow both populations to share their special foods? If the church draws people internationally or multi-ethnically, are there integrated groups where people can get to know each other and share their various foods?

Food can draw people together in group settings. Make people feel welcome. Whether food is catered or people in the groups provide the food (from covered dish to one or several people providing a meal), use the food to bring people together and to converse about the food and what the food means to each other. Food talk is a great way to get people to know each other better in the church in the

Lord. The key is to experiment, try a fellowship group with food, and see what happens.

Board Meetings

There are clearly more types of experiments churches should try in the in-between time of the interim. If a church board does not know how to end its meetings (they go on and on and on), experiment with time limits for reports and action items. Those limits should be realistic, but also absolute. I have tried this at several churches, and the result has been dynamic. People ordinarily stay within the limits and become much better organized in presenting what they have to say and do. The boards then meet for a more reasonable amount of time.

One experimental tool that political organizations use that church officials should use more, especially when personnel and other nonpublic matters need to be discussed, is going off the record. Go into executive session, and no notes are taken, but no action is taken either until you go public. There are times things and people need to be discussed openly, candidly, and honestly. In open meetings this can rarely be done because we do not want to hurt people's feelings. However, do not use this to avoid facing controversy or to keep everything secret. Remember what I said in the chapter on the freedom to explain. And when you come back on record, be prepared tactfully to explain what you are doing and why you are taking the actions. Also, be open for feedback and those who disagree with you. A good interim can easily introduce this to a church that has not tried it before.

Christian Education

If the curricula you are using no longer cut it, consider trying out a different approach. A number of churches have gone to the rotation model. Look it up if you are not familiar with it. Because of the success of Vacation Bible School, more churches are looking at following that model for Sunday school. However, church publishing companies are producing a wide variety of curricula based on solid research of what works best in church settings, and some can be tried for a period to see if they will work with your youth. Do not be obsessed with one and only one curriculum. Sometimes different curricula will be required for different ages.

Many are the times a church needs an interim to help the Christian education program to redevelop or renew itself. It is not necessary for an interim to be a Christian education specialist, but it is helpful if the interim is knowledgeable about what is available and the strengths and weaknesses of various materials. Even more, the interim should be willing and able to work intensely with those in Christian education to lead them to experiment for the sake of those being educated in the faith. See what works and keep it; discard what does not work. It takes experimentation to discover which is which.

Worship

Possibly the most difficult and often most necessary area to experiment is with worship. Unless the service is absolutely set in stone (several high liturgical churches would fit into this category), experimenting with worship is a gift and a freedom the interim has. The fact is that the concept of worship has changed over time, and even how to do the most basic elements of worship has changed over time. For example, while there are hymns that have stood the test of time, recent years have seen an explosion in new hymn writing and new types of hymns. The best way to find out if any of these new hymns fit into the church is to try them, experiment with them, use them at least once, maybe occasionally, and see what takes with the congregation and what does not. Of course, it may involve purchasing a copyright license to allow you to use the new hymns, unless the church buys a new hymnal that has some of them in it. Do honor copyright laws; the alternatives are costly financially and legally.

Do also remember that a number of older hymns have been rediscovered in recent years. These usually do not need copyright permission. I expect many of them are just now being reintroduced to churches, and thus, most people are unfamiliar with them. Consider as emerging churches are doing combining really old hymns with newer hymns. By the way, nineteenth century hymns do not constitute really old; many that do go back to the early days of the church up through the Middle Ages (and possibly some in the Reformation times).

Beyond hymns, what is the church choir doing musically these days? Is it singing only one type of music? Would the choir be open to trying different types of music? The same goes for praise bands because even they can become so oriented to certain types of praise music that after a while, it sounds the same. Nowadays, there are churches that have jazz services, bluegrass services, country services, rock services featuring the music of certain particular rock musicians (U2 is particularly popular), gospel services, barbershop services, even Broadway services, as well as some remarkable classical music services. The fact is Christian music comes in all sizes and shapes these days, and a good musician will find Christian elements in all of the above-mentioned types of music. Try out one or more of these types of services and see what happens.

Again because an interim is transitory, the interim can experiment with these services and special music styles. By exposing the congregation to types of music in worship it has never used before, it allows the congregation to sense the depth and variety of musical styles that make up worship in our world. Even without going fully into one of those types of services, there are usually times during the year certain musicians who specialize in these areas could sing during the worship service or at a special time set aside for them. Look for such musicians and invite them to share their worship with the congregation. Yes, there will be a cost to bring these professionals into your church, but if they demonstrate well their types of music, they will allow the congregation to see a new dimension to worship. Who knows if just that seed will blossom mightily because the interim was willing to experiment!

Jesus said the seed will spread on all types of soil, and the results will be varied depending on the soil, meaning how it is received and whether it can be received. Be open to being the seed bearer for the gift of God to enhance worship in the congregation. Experimentation allows seeds to grow and flourish, especially with worship and music.

We are back to the basic issue: Is worship worship or not? Whatever enhances worship and speaks to the people about God, whom they worship in Jesus Christ, is central to how worship should be. Call this the Holy Spirit leading the church to grow in worship. I have seen both liturgical and free churches worship in ways that really did not do much for the people in their faith journeys and how they experienced how to worship God in Jesus Christ. If it doesn't, it doesn't. The issue then becomes how to make worship truly be worship again. The interim must be willing to lead the congregation in experimenting with the worship to find what really clicks.

Structure

Beyond worship, churches may need to experiment with their structure. If a church is having financial issues, for example, it may be necessary for the interim to propose a business solution, namely, combining jobs. I am seeing a large number of denominational bodies doing this at various levels, and it may well be necessary for the local congregation under financial circumstances. Experiment with combining secretary and treasurer functions, if both previously had been paid positions. If volunteers cannot handle janitorial functions, combine them with someone else's functions or with several staff 's positions. One larger church combined its youth director with its praise leader position, and it worked out brilliantly. It may be necessary to cut hours or develop alternative strategies to ensuring work is done, but with a lesser staff. Bigger churches may have to reduce pastoral staff or combine positions. Certain interims can work part-time and offer the model of the tent-maker pastorate, which a number of churches will have to consider. Similarly, retired pastors working as interims can work at a reduced cost to the church because of retirement pension rules. Some churches seeing this may be open to that model for the subsequent minister.

How is the church doing at getting volunteers to fill positions? If the church is not doing well, it may be time to consider reducing the numbers needed to fill positions. Or it may mean reducing the committees, task forces, and other working groups in the church. Their functions may need to be combined, streamlined, merged, or just simply eliminated. Consider the pool of the workers, says the interim, and then have only the number of groups that match the pool of workers.

It is very easy to double up, triple up, even quadruple up those who work in the church. The same people get stuck with doing many and sometimes the same jobs seemingly forever. That is not fair to them; it does cause burnout for most. Save the church the hassle of losing people who were forced to be overcommitted. Many will walk away, and the church will be worse off. Do not overwhelm people with jobs in the church. If that is happening, cut the positions. It is better to do less with good people than do badly with just a few people doing everything. Experiment and find out what works in the church without consuming people by their doing beyond their capabilities.

On the other side, it may be necessary to expand and experiment with what that means for the church. Extra services or special services may be warranted, but rather than rush into them, experiment with them first. See what works when and how. Otherwise, if one staff member is part-time and the work is more, it may be time to look at full-time, or at least experiment with additional hours and see if they are needed or not.

Is the church keeping up technologically? It may be helpful to experiment with technologies, whether computer programs that need to be upgraded and learned anew or new systems of lighting or printing or cleaning or teaching. Technology is constantly changing, and it is worthwhile to experiment with what is out there and see if it can be adapted for the church's use. This does not mean buying everything out there, but rather find ways to try them out before purchasing. Experiment with the latest. What makes sense will fit in; what does not can be discarded before it becomes a problem.

Understanding Experimenting

Experimenting at its most basic is trying out something new or different to see if it makes a difference for the church. Revitalization and renewal can often come only with experimentation. Trying to push things on people, however, without letting them try such out to see if they really work is a recipe for disaster. Such a technique does not honor the congregation; it does not take the congregation seriously. I have said before that churches are unique and special unto themselves. An interim who does not honor that is an interim who fails a church. Further, an interim who forces changes on a church that a church is not ready for will wind up dividing the church or creating chaos within a church. People may withdraw both themselves and their money and, in worst-case scenarios, will push the interim out of the church.

People need to see and feel and experience a difference and then determine whether they can claim it. Ideally, such experiments should come from the congregation itself. If that is not possible, then the interim should institute them and explain they are temporary, they are experiments, and we want to see what works and what does not work. No interim should insist on experiments without vetting them, without making clear what is involved and how they may help if they work out.

As people try something they have not done before, how do people react to it? Do people get emotional or even irrational about it? Or are they willing to see what happens? Sometimes the interim will have to be a calming experience to people who cannot understand why things cannot stay the same as they have always been. Even an experiment spooks them. It is here that good pastoral techniques and the constant repetition that this is an experiment with a short lifespan are necessary. They have to be assured that it is but an experiment.

In Conclusion

Having said that though, some experiments do become permanent. They are found to be worthwhile and necessary. Until the experiment is tried though, no one will know for sure. An interim should help the church to experiment and encourage the congregation to evaluate the experiment fairly and constructively. The interim will be neutral about the experiments, but the interim will lead the congregation to experiment fruitfully. There are things to be tried, and by trying them, the congregation will see what is needed and what works for the congregation.

The freedom to experiment is a gift the interim can offer to a congregation. Done properly, decently, and in good faith, it allows the congregation to renew itself and find itself and see where it needs to go.

11

The Freedom to Leave

This whole book is premised on the freedom of the interim to leave. An interim is not tied to a church, nor is the interim making a long-term commitment to the church. An interim by definition is an interim, someone who fills in during the interim when there is no permanent, installed, regular pastor or clergy in place. That is the classical understanding of an interim.

Interims without the Name

However, over the course of my ministry, I have discovered that certain churches or denominations that do not have interims per se will put specialized clergy into situations where interims ordinarily function. Thus, as an example in both Catholic and Methodist churches, which put a new pastor in immediately following the departure of the previous pastor, I have seen particular clergy put into situations where the previous pastor failed or had personal issues. These particular pastors had been trained in how to deal with the problems of the previous pastor. More, these pastors or clergy were never long-term holders of the position. They came in to clean up and move on to their next assignment. That is interim in all but name.

Indeed, I could go on with all types of cases where the denomination put clergy into a church setting where the church itself had problems. The role of that pastor was to clean up the messes, whether caused by the church itself or by someone in the church or by the previous pastor. These pastors may not say they are only there for a limited time, but they are. By virtue of the denominational rules, they could not say they were interims because the rules do not allow interims. Yet if it acts like an interim and does everything an interim does and stays only for a limited time, it is an interim, even if the name is unattached.

Usual Leaving

Therefore, consider the value of the freedom to leave that the interim has. In the first place, the interim can leave theoretically at any time. However, typically, interims are hired for a time by a contractual arrangement. Yet even with the most legal obligations to stay a particular time, there is always the opt out, meaning under certain circumstances the interim will leave. The interim most commonly leaves when a new pastor is called, usually sometime before the new minister takes up the position. Nonetheless, there are exceptions to the rule, and an interim could and will leave earlier if certain results happen.

It is not uncommon for an interim to leave after a period of time when the church has made little or no progress in finding the permanent clergy. There are churches that get comfortable with their interims and slow the process down to doing almost nothing. An astute interim will recognize that and leave. The interim is to be temporary, not permanent or even semipermanent, and attempts to do otherwise must be met by a firm response, the freedom to leave before a new pastor is called. Often that is what it takes to get the church moving again in looking for a new pastor.

On the other side, there are times interims have to leave to take care of themselves. This may sound selfish, but interims are human beings with human needs, and there are times those human needs have to be met. The interims may develop health problems that are severe enough to warrant leaving a position. The interim may have family issues that need to be taken care of. The interim may simply burn out in the position and, as such, can no longer function in the situation. Worst of all, the interim finds himself or herself proverbially in over their head. What the interim expected to deal with turns out to be more complex than anticipated and beyond the capability of the interim per se. Thus, the interim leaves. These are some of the times it is good to leave for the sake of the interim and the sake of the church. The freedom of the interim to leave makes leaving for human needs worthwhile.

Suggestion

At the opposite side, there comes a time for the interim to leave, the necessary leaving before the new minister arrives. Unfortunately, there are no real guidelines on when or how this happens. Everyone knows it happens, but going beyond that fact leaves even the most practiced interim a bit befuddled. It becomes a best guess as to when the interim should leave before the new minister arrives.

My suggestion (and this is no hard-and-fast rule) is that the interim should leave about a month before the new pastor is to arrive. This gives the church a bit of time to adjust to a change, and the interim is gone for a time before the new pastor arrives. Thus, when the new pastor arrives, there are no complications of what to do with the interim. This suggestion may need to be modified depending on the denomination's rules or because of certain factors at play in the local church.

Having said that, I can see all types of exceptions. The interim who really needs to work and make a paycheck may need to leave sooner to accommodate a new church position. Church positions do not always wait on what is convenient for the church the interim is presently serving. The interim has to have the freedom to leave sooner if necessary for the interim's financial well-being.

Yogi Berra

Not every new pastor is going to arrive at a schedule always convenient to the interim. The fact is that the interim has to be looking for a new position prior to the new pastor arriving. The interim may try to hold off going to the new church as long as possible, but as long as possible may not be as long as the present church would like. Even more problematic is when during the process of finding a new pastor, the group or persons responsible for doing so informs the interim a new pastor is on the way. At that point, the interim has to move fast, but too often in such situations, the pastor is not on the way as soon as the group thought the pastor would be. If the interim bases moving on the suggested timeline for the new pastor the committee erroneously predicts, the church can be without an interim for some time.

I know for myself and for other interims I have dealt with that there have been times based on what I was told and others were told about the coming pastor that things did not work out. In other words, as Yogi Berra once said, "It ain't over until it's over." The best-laid plans go astray. The group calling the new pastor figures it has everything in place, and then complications arise. The spouse does not want to come. The financial arrangements cannot be worked out. At the last moment, somebody found something out about the new pastor that disqualifies the person. Even the unpredictable can occur, like family emergencies, accidents, disasters, etc. Any imaginable situation can so happen as to make things difficult, if not impossible for the pastor to either come on schedule or come at all.

The interim cannot be bound by those situations. It is unfair to the interim to cancel moving plans because something did not work out. I said the time when the interim leaves is a guess, a best guess at that. Yet it does not always work out. The interim has to have the freedom to leave at such occasions. Admittedly, it leaves a church in a lurch, and alternatives may have to be found. Nonetheless, that is part and parcel of what it means to a church to have an interim. The interim has the freedom to leave.

Why?

Getting back to the basic premise of this book that the freedom to leave is essential to an interim, let me point out what this means. By virtue of being able to leave, as I have pointed out before, the interim is not tied to the church. The interim is not identified with the church. Everyone knows the interim will be leaving at some point in time.

People identify a church with its pastor. It is the church that such and such pastors. No doubt this can cause issues if people do not separate the church from the pastor because for them when the pastor leaves the scene, it is no longer a church. Just go back and read in 1 Corinthians to see the impact such a view had on the church and how Paul had to combat that view.

Despite the negatives of the church being identified with the pastor, Christians readily recognize the value of a regular pastor in a church setting. It provides continuity. The people can work on a longer time arrangement with a pastor than with an interim. The clergy is "permanent" and is not just in and out like the interim. The church can move forward under the pastor in place with that pastor's guidance, direction, and ongoing support.

The interim being transitory makes it possible for a church to define what it is they want in a regular pastor. They understand the difference between here today and gone tomorrow versus staying with us for some years to come. The interim's very presence forces that distinction. They understand the need for continuity and what it will take to ensure that continuity. They work to make it possible for the new clergy to be what they want and what they need because the interim's freedom to leave makes that possible.

They see the limited presence of the interim and realize the necessity of having a longer term existence with the pastor. The interim is a person who by nature cannot get as close to the people as the pastor does, especially if the pastor is around for a fair amount of time. As an example, a pastor who spends twenty to thirty years in a congregation lives through a generation of the people, and that one is known intimately by the people. Such a one has been there for births, confirmations, graduations, marriages, retirements, and even deaths. The people thus turn to this one as they seek and need the church and its services. This one truly is their pastor.

It is just not the same with the interim. The interim's freedom to leave and ultimately the necessity to leave ensures the interim can only relate to people in a specific time and a specific setting, whereas the church lives for those clergy who are not defined by a specific time and a specific setting. As an example, I know churches that keep meticulous records of their pastorates. They may include them in official church history books. They have pictures of them. In oral and visual ways, they focus on their pastors. Sometimes they name something in the church after a pastor. They keep the name of the pastor alive long after that person has died. The clergy are so identified with the church that the church cannot talk about itself apart from the clergy.

This does not happen with interims. They at their best are genuinely appreciated and accepted. Some churches that have hanging photographs or paintings of their pastors will include the interim, especially if the interim made a difference and was particularly appreciated. Yet even these will include the dates of the service, and anyone looking at the pictures will immediately turn to the pictures of those who stayed for some time. The church and its people recognize the value of longer pastorates to the church, and interims clearly do not fit that pattern.

Implications

Someone who has an ego will soon realize that an interim is a humbling experience. Once the interim leaves, the ties to the former church are eliminated. The interim cannot intrude in, influence, or otherwise affect what is going on in the church thereafter. Even if by some happenstance, the interim hears of bad news about the church after departing, the interim cannot get involved. If confronted and having to say something, the interim has to reply by telling whomever to contact the denominational or other officially appropriate people. Having done that, walk away. You have to realize your limitations and your role with all humility, or you will not be an effective interim.

The freedom to leave means the freedom to leave totally. It is not a partial leaving. You leave means exactly that—you leave. You have nothing to do with the church. You are not part of the church. The church served a role for you to work, and if you did it well, you can leave graciously and happily. Yet you have done your job, and the job is over. Therefore, this church is no longer your concern. It is no longer part of your job. Your role with the church is finished, period.

Emotionally, that is hard to hear. After all, ministers are human beings too. We develop emotional ties, even in temporary situations. Sometimes, we develop friendships. And if when we leave, people thank us and make it clear they appreciate us, it becomes harder for us to let go. Nonetheless, we must. We are there to make it possible for churches to move on to the next step, the new regular pastor, and our freedom to leave makes that possible. We cannot be a hindrance to that process; our purpose is to expedite that process. We leave. We go. We cut our ties to the church and place them in God's hands, knowing God used us for the good of the church.

I do not want this to be a naïve chapter. I am aware of denominations that allow an interim to become the regular minister. As a personal note, I feel that is a bad idea because it is the very condition of the interim to be free to leave and be a transitory figure. An interim with the freedom to leave does not build a personal tie to the local congregation. An interim with the freedom to leave is able to withstand the angst a congregation must undergo before it can move on. An interim with the freedom to leave is able to do more than a regular clergy. An interim with the freedom to leave can bring about changes that an ordinary clergy cannot. An interim with the freedom to leave can effectively deal with problem people, instead of leaving them for somebody else or else waiting for them to die.

Having said all of that, some people will no doubt point to the business or school models, among others, whereby an interim is brought in either as a trial or for emergency purposes and then is hired as the new head. Of course, even in those models, there are some interims that are truly interims. They are called to that position and then leave when the new permanent person is brought aboard. These are people usually within the organization who are known for their ability to help out, and once done, they go back to their regular duties.

Yet when an interim in such a situation assumes the full-time position, it is commonly because someone within the organization really knows the organization. These are people who have lived and worked within the organization often for a number of years. The organization really does not want to go outside of itself for its effective regulars. That is a significant difference between organizational interims and church interims, which are trained to be professional "outsiders."

The need for an outsider is at the crux of the interim in a church position. This is a person who brings an outside perspective to a church situation wherein people cannot and will not see the obvious problems. By being an outsider, that person is free to analyze a situation fairly and objectively and then act upon what needs to be acted upon. The interim as an outsider remains an outsider by virtue of not assuming the full position. To lose that outsider status and become an insider thereby limits what the interim can and will do.

I do realize there are exceptions to everything. Thus, certain interims are true outsiders brought in to the business or educational world to see if they would fit. If not, they are let go. If so, they are adopted into the system and become the positions they held temporarily. And yes, there are churches that would love to adopt their interims. They are perceived as fitting into their system, and the church does not want to look further or consider that a new regular pastor is what a church needs. It is easy on the church, and it is easy on the interim.

Unfortunately, for an interim to become the regular pastor defeats the very concept of interim for a church. It is necessary for a space and time to allow a church to think through what it wants and what it needs. The interim can experiment. The interim can evaluate and change. The interim can act without repercussions. The interim can be an interim by virtue of not having to look over the shoulder to see if the position will be offered to this one. If the interim is aiming for the position, the interim is going to do what it takes to get the position and will not be doing what is required of an interim. The church will simply not be prepared for what is coming next because the interim aiming for the position is not going to do the interim work that needs to be done.

In Conclusion

I say this emphatically: the freedom to leave makes the interim an interim, indeed makes it possible for the interim to act as an interim. Elsewise, the necessary work of the interim goes by the wayside because the one in the position is self-serving instead of church-serving. The freedom to leave is at the crux of being an interim. The interim will come and go after a while when it is time to move on. The interim will make the church the necessary church for the new pastor. Don't be an interim if you reject the freedom to leave.

12

The Freedom to Hope

I have saved the freedom to hope for the last chapter. This is the very theological basis of an interim. An interim by the grace of God provides hope for the church. There is a future. There is a hope for a new beginning with a new pastor. Seeing this temporary, transitory, short-termed person filling the pulpit reminds me that something more is coming. God is using this person to make it possible for every "me" of the congregation to say a new day is coming. Hope is shown in the presence and work of the interim.

Of course, I could have used the freedom to hope as the very first chapter. Since hope is the whole basis for an interim's work, it could be the introduction to the whole book. It is on the basis of hope that the interim is called, and on that basis the interim makes it possible for the church to move forward.

The Faith to Hope

The faith to hope makes the interim's work possible. It does take faith to be able to believe in hope, to imagine hope, to experience hope, and to make hope come alive. Thus, the interim has to have a strong-enough faith to see the hope and enable the hope to live. The interim knows where the hope goes, but that hope is built on a faith that this is where God wants me to be.

I come into each interim position led by faith. I am convinced God wants me in this particular place at this particular time, in order that hope may live for the people I am about to serve. I pray about each position. I carefully research each position. I want to be absolutely sure God wants me here. I will listen to others talking about the church and be sure they see me there. If it is God's will, I will be there, and I will provide the hope the church needs.

This freedom to hope lives in faith, depends upon faith, and derives from faith. I am convinced I am in the interim ministry because God has led me there. God sees in me the type of person who, through faith, enables hope. Considering that hope has become a central theme in certain theological circles and with particular theologians, it is vital interim ministers understand how this wonderful Christian hope is basic to the interim.

Thus, in a true Christian paradox, hope builds up faith. The hope I offer as an interim minister makes it possible for those whom I serve to have faith and live in faith. The faith sustains them. They see hope displayed, and they know their faith is real. God has brought the interim to them, and that presence shows them that their faith matters. No matter what they have endured before or what has happened to their previous pastor, God has not given up on them. God is still with them. Their faith is upheld indeed by the hope provided by the interim.

Promises of Hope

Hope is assumed, taken for granted, even considered natural in a normal pastorate. Yet when things go awry, hope is often the first casualty. I have heard many church people express pure hopelessness prior to or shortly after my arrival. They despair. They feel abandoned by God. They wonder if they have a future. Therefore, I have to reassure them. I have to let them know there is hope and God is still present. Yes, God is leading them to a new future, even if it feels like the wandering in the wilderness time for a while.

Yes, the people of Israel knew what the wilderness was about. Yet when all was said and done, they eventually made it to the Promised Land. Later, the people would be sent into exile, and they had to be told there was hope even in a foreign land. More, eventually they could hope they would return to the Promised Land, and they did. The whole concept of a promised land is built on a hope, a hope that there would be a promised land, in which a land would be given to them as promised by God. The people had to trust God to ensure the hope would live. They had to have faith, but with that faith hope lived. Even at their worst of times, hope remained. The ability to hope kept a people alive and ensured there was a great future with God.

Eventually, that hope would lead to the promise of the Christ, the coming of the Lord. No one knew when he would come, but come he did. It was another promise by God for the future, and people had to have the faith needed to keep that hope alive. In God's time, the hope was realized in Jesus Christ. As an interim, I need to stoke that hope, reclaim that hope, and show that because of the faith of others, that hope was realized.

Jesus Christ to the church and in the interim setting crucially is the proclamation of that hope then but also now and into the future. God will be with the people to the end of the age and then into eternity itself because of the hope delivered in Jesus Christ. This is why Advent sermons can speak to interim situations. It is why Easter starts with one resurrection and points to a future resurrection. In the meantime, we live in light of the cross and resurrection in hope, and that is where interims lead the people.

Hope Fulfilled

Once hope is realized, hope is supported. People buy into hope when they see hope fulfilled. One of the great gifts of an interim is that congregations can see hope fulfilled when the new pastor arrives. The hope the interim gives is now brought to realization in the presence of the new pastor. The hope that was shown in the interim is now known to be true.

Once that hope is seen as true, it opens the way to allowing hope for the long term. In other words, seeing hope's promises fulfilled on a short-term basis allows for hope on the long-term. Thus, the Christian seeing the promise of hope coming true with a new pastor can more fully see the hope of eternity with the Lord and the final resurrection. What appears to be a little thing like an interim ending successfully makes it possible for seeing the Lord at work in people's lives and in history as well.

Because the Lord made possible a successful interim, I can claim this to see the hope that sustains me in my life. I will hold on to that as one example of how God works to know God will be with me all the days of my life. God will be with my church, and God will be with me, and I can hope for life after death with the Lord. It is one more hope shown to be true that I can use for the hope that comes with my death.

Further, by seeing a hope fulfilled after a time, I can look forward in hope to when the Lord returns again. The hope of the interim helps to reinforce the hope of Jesus's return. The interim becomes one more building block to make me and others like me look forward to the return of Jesus Christ. It may or it may not be in my or anybody now living's lifetime, but Jesus will come again. That is the hope we have, and with the hope seen in the interim, we are more convinced of that ultimate hope.

Short-term hopes fulfilled enhance and make possible long-term hopes yet to be. We all need something realized to make hope live beyond ourselves. We do not want false hopes, delusions, self-deceptions, and unrealistic dreams. We want hope built on a firm foundation. We want hope that is true. We want hope that sustains us. We want hope that lives in us. We want hope to make a difference in our lives and in the world. We want hope seen to be true to lead us to the greatest hope that will come. This is the theological gift an interim brings to people in the congregation.

Hope lives. Hope has a home. Hope makes a difference. Hope is in a remarkable God way partially incarnate in the interim. Obviously, hope is fully incarnate in Jesus Christ, who is the hope of the world and the hope of the peaceable kingdom.

Hope in Scripture

Indeed, chapter 11 of Isaiah ties together for Christians the Christ and the ultimate peaceable kingdom. It starts by saying, "A shoot shall come out from the stump of Jesse." After going into a fuller description of what this individual will be like (and Christians have always identified this picture with Jesus), immediately we hear, "The wolf shall live with the lamb, the leopard shall lie down with the kid, the calf and the lion and the fatling together, and a little child shall lead them." More details of the peaceable kingdom are given, concluding with "For the earth will be full of the knowledge of the

Lord as the waters cover the sea." The hope of the Christ makes the hope of the peaceable kingdom and the Lord real.

That is just one among many passages in Scripture that detail hope, and interim pastors should preach them, recite them, say them, and otherwise make these texts live for the congregation. Let the congregation hear the hope. Whether it is in Psalms talking about hoping in the Lord or his word (see, e.g., Psalm 42:5, 11; 43:5; 62:5; 65:5; 119:43, 49, 81, 114, 116, 147, 166), Jeremiah's oft-quoted "plans I have for you…to give you a future with hope" (Jer. 29:11), Lamentations' remarkable hope amid the total destruction and conquest of a people of God (Lam. 3:21, 24, 29), and the real dialogue about hope that dominates the book of Job (read chapters 3–8, 11, 14, 17, 19 and God's answer in chapter 41), hope is a constant theme in the Old Testament.

Christians are called to hope in the New Testament. Paul in his epistles, as well as stories about Paul in Acts (Acts 23:6, 24:15, 26:6–7, 28:20), insists upon hope. Much of Romans builds on hope (see chapters 4, 5, 8, and 15, plus 12:12). The famous paean to love in 1 Corinthians 13 ends with the three that remain, with love the greatest, but hope is one of the three. This hope lives in 2 Corinthians (1:10, 13; 3:12), Galatians (5:5), Ephesians (1:12, 4:4), Colossians (1:5, 23, 27), 1 Thessalonians (1:3, 4:13, 5:8), 2 Thessalonians (2:16), 1 Timothy (1:1, 4:10), and Titus (1:2, 2:13, 3:7). Beyond Paul, consider Hebrews (3:6; 6:11, 18–19; 7:19; 10:23), the great new birth into a living hope of 1 Peter (1:3, but also in the book see 1:13, 21; 3:15), and 1 John (3:3). In the Gospel of Matthew, Jesus fulfills the prophecy of Isaiah, providing hope for the Gentiles (12:21). Those are just passages that actually use the word *hope*. The concept is embedded in the New Testament.

Embedded Hope

Use these passages. Embed these passages into the very core of the congregation. These verses and their ilk should become so embedded in the congregation that the people live unto hope in Jesus Christ. That hope embedded by the interim becomes part of what the congregation is and will be. That embedded hope guides the congregation as it moves forward to a new pastorate.

The interim needs to be embedded hope. Just as journalists embed with soldiers in battle during times of war to fully understand and report properly what the soldiers are facing, the interim is embedded with the congregation in its battle to move forward. The interim is embedded hope for Christians in their ongoing battles. To fully understand and report properly what God is doing in Jesus Christ by the Holy Spirit in this congregation, the interim embeds hope to a people of God.

We choose to hope. Hope is not automatic. We all know people who, because of disasters, accidents, losses, and other bad times give up on hope. Jesus's famous parable about the sower (Matthew 13:1–9, 18–23 or Mark 4:1–9, 13–20 or Luke 8:4–8, 11–15) always rings painfully true. The seed sown on rocky ground are those who hear the word with joy, but when trouble, persecution, or testing come about, they fall away. People too often give up on hope when bad things happen to them. We have to choose to have hope and hear the end of that parable that these sown in good soil will bear fruit because they accept, understand, and hold fast to the word.

In Conclusion

Interims to be effective choose to have hope. It is a choice. We choose to have hope. It is a free choice. We have the freedom to choose hope or not. Interims freely choose hope and live that hope, embed that hope, incarnate that hope, and ensure that hope for a congregation. They make that hope come alive for people who give in to hopelessness, despair, loss, fear, anxiety, and so much else that makes it hard to see God at work in their lives. Interims have the freedom to hope, and that reality of hope makes the interim effective.

This is no delusional hope. This is hope based on Jesus Christ and a church where there genuinely is the need for hope. There are situations in churches where the future is not hopeful. Money, membership, and location may conspire against a church's future, so that the hope that is real is only for a gentle ending. There are special pastors who can lead churches through death itself, the death of a church.

However, an interim is not designed to lead people to death in the Lord, but rather life in the Lord and life abundantly. The freedom

to hope is to ensure there will be a good future in the Lord for the church. The freedom to hope is to provide for the promise of a new pastor to work with the congregation after the interim is gone. The freedom to hope is to allow a congregation to see hope at work and hope realized. The freedom to hope is to be the living tool in faith of the interim. By virtue of the interim's freedom to hope, the church lives its life in the Lord and its life abundantly indeed.